LIFE AFTER HIM

STARTING OVER AFTER HIGH-CONFLICT RELATIONSHIPS

MYRNA IVETTE CLAUDIO, EVANGELIST AND LIFE COACH

Difference Press

Washington, DC, USA

Published 2022

DISCLAIMER

Cover Design: Jennifer Stimson

Editing: Cory Hott

Author Photo Courtesy of Attreo Santayana, LinkedInHeadshotsNYC.com

"*Life After Him* will be immensely helpful to both men and women around the world, which have had difficult relationships, divorce, or loss. This book encompasses everything one needs to know about relationships. When we fall into a relationship, we do it believing that this is going to be the best for us. As time goes on, one finds out that it might be true, or we could have made the worst decision of our lives. After reading this book, it not only gave me hope and inspiration, but the realization that I could be my best self. Whatever happens, whether in a relationship or on my own, I am still the best person who I am supposed to be, giving not only to myself, but giving what I learned to others. In essence, I took out of this book, that you do not have to be in a relationship to fulfilled and be the best version of yourself that you can be fulfilled."

— LUCILLE MCLEOD, LICENSED CLINICAL
SOCIAL WORKER, LCSW

"I am very delighted that God's esteemed elect lady has decided to open her personal story and pen and these timeless experiences for all and posterity. I have known evangelist Myrna for many years of productive and fruitful ministry touching countless of hungry souls including myself. She exudes a poetic and prophetic perspective in her teachings and coaching platform. Her qualities I believe will help the readers to get in touch with their hidden personal pains, frustration and gain much needed healing. The author is also very frank and down to earth. Other times, she is simply hilarious. Readers will enjoy great depth of understanding and no boring moment in her no-holds-barred style. Myrna has spoken in length at our church."

— DR. PATRICK ODIGIE, PRESIDENT OF
PATRICK ODIGIE EVANGELISTIC MISSIONS
(POEM)

CONTENTS

A Note from the Author xi

1. Blind and in Love 1
   Abide 7
2. Trusting the Process 9
   On Eagles' Wings 29
3. The World Is Your Oyster 31
   Be Free My Love 45
4. Insecurity and Identity Crisis 47
   Your Inner Being 57
5. Growing Love Pains 59
   A Flower 75
6. The Roots of Abandonment and Forgiveness 77
   I Am 87
7. Determined to Be in the Winner's Circle 89
   My Sunshine 99
8. On the Other Side of the Moon 101
   The Salvation Prayer 107
   Rain 115
9. Finding the One True Love 117
   Silence 131
10. Girl, Straighten Your Crown 133
    Queen of Ages 145
11. The Door to Your Destiny Awaits 147
    Country Girl Arising 159
12. Love Awakening – My Knight in Shining
    Armor 161

In a Distance 181
Acknowledgments 183
About the Author 195
About Difference Press 197
Other Books by Difference Press 199
Thank You 201

I lovingly dedicate this book to my sons Ronald Edward, Leonard Stephen Anthony, and Michael Sean. Your love and support throughout this process, and always, touches the very core of my heart. Since you were all born, you stole my heart, and it became forever yours. My boys, now men, you are the reason I live, breath and have my being. I thank God that you did not allow my life's experiences to affect you, but instead, you chose the road to never allow what happened to me, happen to you, and you have made sure, that you now have thriving and healthy relationships. Always remember to work hard, play harder, be strong, courageous, to follow the light, to live in peace, joy, unity, and harmony with each other, and humanity. My sons, the world is your oyster! I love you more, more, more than coffee, and forever into infinity.

— Mama Marina

A NOTE FROM THE AUTHOR

Poetry and scriptures are found in the pages of this book as droplets of love, sprinkled with fairy dust, sugar, honey, sweetness, cherries, chocolate, and loving care, like the dew of the morning. Here is a love letter to my reader…

— Myrna Ivette Claudio

1

BLIND AND IN LOVE

The pain in our lives can be mild, or extremely intense. It can blind us and if we find love, it can bring us the wrong kind of love. It is important to dig deep into the pain we are encountering, which does cost time and even more pain. Relationships can sometimes be good, but sometimes exceedingly difficult. We must learn to trust in our intuition and become the masters or directors of our movie. We are at times thrown around like a ping pong ball, back and forth.

In the pages of this book, we will learn to take authority of our lives and our wellbeing, and no longer allow these relationships to rule and reign over us. We will explore avenues and perspectives into not being so blind, but being alert and aware, this will allow us to become keener and more aware of our surroundings, with ourselves, and the outside world, and individuals. It is called wisdom. "Wisdom is the principal thing," the Bible declares. Many of us have education, knowledge, street smarts, but lack wisdom. Wisdom is the gift from God, and the Universe, to show us how to use the knowledge, the book-smart capacity. Wisdom is more precious than rubies. It is the spiritual gift that shows us what to do with all the book knowledge and all we learned in books, in school, colleges and universities. You can have all the knowledge in the world, but if you lack wisdom on how to use the knowledge, you lack the greatest gift given to humanity.

I want to begin with the story of Marianna Hicks, forty-two, part-time working mom of two. Marianna is one of those hot and sexy moms, who loves her image, and believes she is the queen of her castle. Her home is impeccable, her children dressed to the tee for school, and she considers herself a trophy wife and mother. She lives in Dallas, Texas. She is outgoing, and loves her family, but enjoys her time out with friends, and has an intense collection of trendy cowboy boots.

Marianna had it all: the house, the husband, the children, and the white picket fence. In reality, it was a façade. From the outside looking in, life was perfect. Marianna recently separated. Mind you, this was not her first rodeo. Marianna has a history of broken relationships, and the reason being is she did not know herself. She attracted the wrong kind of men. In her previous marriage, she married a well-to-do company executive, who in all reality, really did not give her the attention she craves or deserves as the mother of his children. She was blind and in love.

Marianna at this point just left her husband, and stormed out of the house, and thank God, her children had a sleep over at her parents'. She had been through enough, and stormed out of the house. Whenever Eric comes home from another business trip – and she has been recently experiencing more verbal abuse from her husband than ever before – she proceeds to go upstairs to their bedroom after cleaning the kitchen after dinner, and he is yelling at her for having some folded clothes on top of the bed which she was going to put away. He made her feel like two pennies waiting for change. Calling her all kinds of names in the book. She proceeded to approach him, and ask him, "Why are you speaking to me like this again? I did nothing to you. It is Friday night, and I brought the kids over to mom and dads, so we can have a nice evening together. All you do is fight with me. You have so much hatred in your eyes." He told her to shut up and threw the keys on the nightstand, almost cutting her eye. She was scared and decided to run and just leave. He had previously shut the door on her the last time he was home on a business trip. She got her purse downstairs, grabbed her keys, and left. She went to her parents, and never looked back.

She always felt he was cheating on her for a long while, and tried to be the perfect wife, have dinner ready, make sure kids were well-behaved, so she was blinded by love. Until fear set her free from a man that did not care for her at all. Eric never once attempted to reach out to her, and she filed for divorce.

As she laid in bed, her thoughts and fears were strong, thinking, "I must carry the burden," concerned about the finances. She was experiencing emotions that range from abandonment, fear, anger, rejection, identity crisis, unforgiveness, lack of self-worth, and insecurities. These emotions as she laid in the bed, were swirling in her head, as she prayed and dozed off into sleep.

The next morning, she calls her best friend, Catherine, and asks if she can come over and bring coffee to talk. They get together at her friend's house, and she shares with Catherine the news of her breakup. She also broke the news to her parents that morning at the kitchen table. Her parents consoled her and said, "We are here for you. Stay as long as you need for you and the children." Which was awesome, as this all happened and transpired out of the blue. At this moment, Catherine asks her, "And the children?" Marianna responded, "They will know soon; I just told them, 'We are having fun with grandma and grandpa for now,' and that dad was on a long business trip. I needed to buy some time to let the kids know what transpired, as I was not returning to that house."

She spends quite a bit of time and shares all with Catherine, and her friend asked her, "What you are most worried about?" She replied, "Being alone, raising my kids alone, and making sure my kids are fine. Thank you, Catherine, for listening to me." She was so shocked last night, especially his tone of voice and the verbal abuse she encountered. He made her question her identity and her self-worth.

She went home. The kids were fine. Everyone went to bed, and she was having trouble sleeping again, feeling the world is now on her shoulders. Her fears right then were, if she does not get herself together, she may end up in depression, and she cannot afford to lose her children. In her words, she said to me, "I must get myself together. Tomorrow I will go to work, as I work part-time, in the library in town. I will find work online. I know I can do something with my fashion sense." Marianna designs jewelry and clothing on the side as a hobby. She did just that. She went to work, and held her head high, as she had been crying for the last couple of days. She went home, got the kids from school, and as they were done with their homework, they decided to play and enjoy themselves. She did her homework online and did her research.

With much research, she has a part-time job, hopefully not for long, and opened a line of clothing, that she had been working on for years, and her line of necklace and bracelet jewelry. She went ahead and set up her online business, and now it is starting to pick up. Day by day, she learns more and more. People love her turquoise jewelry that she makes, and it is really doing well.

I know deep down inside what she desires is to have a drive, her desire is to be happy, and to dance, and sing, although not a professional – her desire to feel alive again is what I am trying to say. She has dealt long enough with broken relationships, divorce, and this is just as about as much as she is going to take. She wants and needs answers, and she will keep praying and believing that her newfound life is coming.

These are her words:

Dreams are around the corner, and new horizons are waiting for. My longing words are what I desire as my dream comes true. My reality is I am seeking answers.

I wish I were doing as well as my business. I am still needing help from abandonment, and rejection issues. My next best thing is to Google self-help books and see if I can find my identity back and get my voice back. My friend Catherine invited me to her home, as some of the girls were doing a book club, and so I am going to join that. My goal and purpose are to find myself, as I have been praying for a way to feel better. I need to find myself; I need to heal; I need restoration of my broken heart. I need to get my identity back and create a new life after leaving my abusive relationship.

"She is clothed with strength and dignity, and she laughs without fear of the future."

— PROVERBS 31:25, NLT

ABIDE

Sit still and be,
Spend time with me
Learn to abide,
In stillness free
Waiting to tell you,
Of all the blessings
To heal you,
And give you lessons
Am always here,
Your inner being
So do not fear,
My love, my dear
I love to show you,
New places to go
Where you will thrive,
And you will grow
Where will life bring you,
You just don't know
Fear not my love,
My queen, my dove, abide in me,

Be still my love
I love you more,
Than you will know.

— MYRNA IVETTE
CLAUDIO

2

TRUSTING THE PROCESS

I can recall that day when my boyfriend was over at the house – I was in high school at the time – when the lusty high school girl was there, Patricia. She was there with all of us in the living room of my home. Our home would be the only place we would be as mom would never ever allow us in other homes. It was our home that had all the kids from school over on the weekend. Ralph decided to be such a gentleman, and walk Patricia to the corner so she would be safe. When they took a while, he looked like he had seen a ghost. Like his life was never the same. This experience was the first experience I felt that originated my insecurities and I questioned this to myself. If you truly like someone – of course, we were young, but I wasn't stupid – why the hell are you taking this girl for a walk? I was so naive. A few years later, he went off to college and mind you, I never heard from him. Years later, I heard he became a rich and successful man, and the stars aligned, or whatever you may want to call that. We saw each other again as grownups after being married with children, and I brought up her name, he excused it as if he didn't remember. But I never forgot. This was the beginning of my so-called teenage love experience.

Years went by and I married as a young girl. Let me tell you, I was too young, I was only eighteen. What the hell did I know. The back of my ears was still wet. I knew nothing except I was cute, pretty, and had a nice home, nice parents and siblings. I married young right after high school. In those days, unfortunately, that's what we did, but I was fortunate. God gave me a beautiful healthy baby boy.

THE HONEYMOON WIFEY

On our honeymoon, we were in a boat with this other honeymoon couple. The wifey, as I call her, was so prudish, with her nose up in the air. I did my best to ignore her, but I was married to Charlie, the one who talks to even the trees when no one is around, like the mayor of the town. So this wifey, said, "What kind of a dress material are you wearing – looks cheap." I said, "I really don't know. Why?" She remarked, "This is my wedding dress material, satin, which I made into a dress for the honeymoon." I said, "Oh, nice." I felt the condemnation, her trying to belittle me. She then blurted out these words, "Must be because you are Puerto Rican. They don't carry this material there." Mind you, I was only eighteen years old, truly, a baby in my own right, off to an island with Charlie, after a huge wedding, and this girl, around my age, spoke to me in this manner.

I was not grown up enough to answer her back; I was more in shock. I shut down and felt like two pennies waiting for change, and even Charlie didn't defend me. I couldn't even defend myself, as I had not enough street smarts, maturity, or wisdom to answer her back. I never said a word, not even to Charlie, but I never forgot that remark, that dark cloud, that abusive tone, from that young bride. It did me harm, when I was innocent and happy and just starting out in life, for someone to be so hurtful about the fact that I am from another country. Little does wifey know, Puerto Rico is a Commonwealth of the United States of America. I mention this to say, this created a deep wound, that I never spoke about, and it trickled into giving me rejection issues in my relationships and in my life. Needless to say, Charlie and I got divorced, with one child, feeling betrayed, abandoned, misunderstood, lied to, and verbally abused in that marriage made me feel unwanted and rejected and unloved, as if I wasn't important enough.

WHEN POVERTY STRIKES

I then on and off had other, smaller relationships, until I met Peter, who was, to say the least, poor, and good look-ing. With Peter, I had more children. We married, and again, felt I just jumped from one relationship to another, like I rebounded. We lived paycheck to paycheck, and I was comfortable in that setting, thinking it was what I deserved, but I knew I deserved better. Deep down in my soul, I knew there was a better life for me and my children. I would be in lines trying to get food, cheese from the government, food stamps, and welfare.

Believe me, I was thankful that my kids had food. My children were our priority, so they were well taken care of. I got babysitting jobs, and when I went into the Welfare Office, I did not complain knowing my children would have food.

For Peter, it was one job after another, and we moved from one placed to the other, such a rollercoaster life. One day he was out working, and my door had no locks, so I couldn't sleep. I felt alone, abandoned, ashamed, and poverty-stricken. I turned to Church, as my out, and went with my children faithfully for years. Peter also went and got closer to God. Still, it was not the kind of life I had dreamed of with this second marriage, and I decided to leave. I was confused, alone, but I knew there was something out there better for me. I was going from relationship to relationship trying to find love but always hit a wall. All I desired was a clear path, a clear direction, but kept letting the experiences in my relationships rule me with pain, rejection, abandonment, loss of self-worth.

DESPERATE TO FIND LOVE

Soon after – you know me, I can't be alone – I finally met me a church man. Hallelujah. I said, "Oh my! So handsome, so kind! Here he is, my knight in shining armor, Mr. Right. All will be well now." This Mr. Right, Jeremy, owns his house, and now I am secure and happy.

The honeymoon phase was great. He has no children. I have three children, things were going nicely. I loved that our bills were paid on time. I never saw not even one of his paychecks, I didn't even care. I was just so happy there was food in the refrigerator, the bills were paid, and we lived in a nice neighborhood. We became a church-going family, not rich, just all in its perfect alignment and order. I was looking for the catch, me and my insecure demons, looking for maybe another woman, maybe he doesn't really love me, always questioning my well-being. By now, my sons are teenagers, and Jeremy worked in the town electrical company, bringing home a nice salary. We both became much involved in the church.

We started a television ministry evangelizing the Gospel of Christ. I then, on my own, was called to teach the Word of God and start a home Bible study. Jeremy, even from the beginning, always went by his mother Ann's, house all the time. He began eating dinner there, spending every waking moment with his mom. I said, damn, now I married a mama's boy, I knew there was a catch. I didn't do too much complaining, as I really had it good, and my boys had a roof over their heads. I found this strange. I kept my mouth shut.

I would go there after work, as I was a housewife, and would meet him there at his mom's. I inquired, of course, to him. He would say, "That's okay. You can spend time with your kids, and I have my room upstairs. I will be home later for bed, and you can always come here and eat dinner with us." I said this is not normal. Being in church life, I quoted the Bible to him, and said in Matthew 19:5 (NKJB) "For this reason a man shall leave his father and mother and be joined to his wife, and the two shall become one flesh." No answer, silence, so I therefore left that night from his mother's house early to think about this. Next day, same thing happened, and continued happening. He would see me if I went there. He was loving and nice, just weird. You can bring a horse to water, but you cannot make the horse drink it. I decided, I wanted my marriage, so I would meet him. Strangely enough, he was always happy to see me, and we went out to dinners, did road trips, strange relationship. He definitely felt a tie to his mom, or worried about leaving her as she was elderly. I don't know what it was but it was not normal, that is for sure!

I stopped trying to figure it out. All I knew was that my kids were in good schools, we were in a good home, eating healthy and prospering. All was great except this dude was a mama's boy to the core. Interestingly enough, his mama was so good to me too. Just super out of the normal range of a normal life. I've told you why I rolled with it, my children. Until one day, Jeremy and I took a ride to the city, and I was the car with him, and he was angry at something or someone and I got the brunt of it. As I spoke, he yelled so loud in the car, he yelled, "Listen, not only do I not love you, and I don't even like you. As far as am concerned, I never want to see you again. I not only never want to see you again, but I also hope to God, I never see you in Heaven, when we go there." I was speechless, startled, I couldn't even talk, my tongue was tied. Jeremy was yelling so loud the verbal abuse was horrific. My heart was in fear as he drove down the city streets on that Saturday morning.

Months went by, he apologized, and after that things were quiet. I was thinking where I would go. I don't have a job, I have still young children, I don't even have a car although I can drive. I began a plan to get my car. Things slowly went back to the way they were; he still never came home, only to sleep, and my children and I had Thanksgiving and Christmas without him. I made it good for me and my children and we celebrated on our own. I went out of my way to give the best holidays to my children. I was not wise at the time, and it was his birthday, so I offered to take him to dinner. He agreed, but he said let's do lunch instead. I said okay, lunch is fine.

It was beautiful sunny day. We went to a nice Italian Restaurant. Finally, Jeremy apologized for his behavior. It was as if he had another personality. At this point, tired of being so alone and independent, I didn't care anymore. So we are at this nice Italian Restaurant and he wants to now go to the park. He tells me in the car, "I am going for a walk." I said, "Can I go with you?" He said, "No, it's okay, I will just be right back." And we are now parked, as he's getting ready to leave me there. Lo and behold, he never came back. I was left alone after lunch – it was like around 2:00 p.m. – and I was alone for hours,

My home was one hour away. I had no car but his car – thank God I still had his keys. I thought to myself, "My children are fine." They were with my mother, and they are so grown up and out with friends. So they were growing up nicely and independent.

What do I do? Do I go looking for him? Maybe he died in the park or passed out and no one knows. Or maybe he met up with a girlfriend for his birthday, or he had a party that I wasn't invited to. Well, I had his car, and he left the keys in the car, so I drove around, nothing, could not find him. Mind you, he was a sick man. At that time, I didn't have a car to go home. Jeremy never returned until 8:00 p.m. I didn't even speak a word to him. I was so mad and angry I was afraid he would flip like he did in the city when he ripped out my heart with words. The feelings that had creeped up were anger. It was building up inside me. I was sick and tired of running after him. I was frustrated, and an incredible sense of abandonment, low self-esteem, and rejection were growing inside of me.

Several months later, Jeremy began complaining about breathing issues and chest pains, and we went to the hospital and was diagnosed with a heart problem which caused him to get heart surgery immediately. He was an ill man not only physically, but I believe emotionally as well. I truly loved him as you can see. I would go out of my way to constantly meet him. I know it was not smart of me, but I was blind and in love.

I have experienced nothing but pain and rejection in my life and relationships and believe me, there's more to tell and unfortunately, this relationship is going in the direction of another breakup due to abuse, abandonment, rejection. Jeremy got worse, and he could not breathe. He called his doctor and was told it may have to be another surgery. Unbelievably enough he may have to have another stent put into his heart. He felt defeated. One night, strangely enough, he said, "Good night. Don't ever forget that I love you." I'm thinking, what the heck is going on with this man. I didn't say a word, and we fell asleep.

SUICIDE ATTEMPT

The next morning comes, and I hear grunting on the floor, as Jeremy is crawling to the bathroom. He had foam coming out of his mouth, he could not speak. He was crawling like a snake. I helped him and pushed him into the bathroom and apparently he wanted to use the toilet to urinate. He was almost non-responsive, but pointing to the toilet bowl. My granddaughter Jessica, only six at the time, was holding him up with me, as I'm calling an ambulance and his family as well. The ambulance came and they took him to the hospital. I told my eldest son to pick up his daughter, my granddaughter. My son did, and I ran to the hospital. I did not know what transpired: a heart attack, something. When I get to the hospital, Jeremy's brother was there. Jeremy woke up and he yelled at brother and said, "What the hell am I doing here in the hospital! You called the ambulance." He said, "No, your wife did." Once he saw me, he yelled and told security to get me out of there. He called the nurse, security came, and, me being the wife, I was escorted off the hospital floor. However, thank God, I was allowed to be in the lobby in the waiting room. We all found out, Jeremy had tried to commit suicide, and I intervened. I didn't know he had tried to commit suicide, and he was livid. What was I supposed to do? I know damn right that I did the correct thing. He would have died.

I was downstairs in the waiting room of the hospital as the family came down to calm me down and all I remember was tears of shock, abandonment, rejection, and confusion all at the same time. They let us know it was a suicide attempt that night at home. That evening, while at the hospital, in his hospital room, they set a guard at his door to make sure he wouldn't attempt another suicide attempt. He drank many Xanax pills to try to kill himself, but it did not work. He lived, and he did not live happily ever after. At this point, I decided when he comes home, I will refrain from bringing him any additional stress or pain. He survived, came home, healed, had another heart surgery, and for the next few years, he continued his same routine, his same life, his same schedule.

Of course, all the while his mom, kept by his side, more than ever. He went back to his regular schedule, back to work, and he's now in the hopes this last surgery worked and he's hoping he can breathe better and for several years it did work out okay for him. As for me, I am coming to a clear and concise understanding: I needed help, and I need to deal with yet another breakup, which is inevitable, but I have gained an understanding that these roots of rejection, abandonment, abuse, anger, fears, cannot take the best of me. I have my children and I needed to come out of this situation, and be a better person, and an example to my children, so that there is healing and growth. I needed to find my identity and source in my life.

Experience is key to being able to help another human being in life as they have gone through crisis or hurts and difficulties. I have experiences in broken relationships, hurts, pain, abandonment, rejection, lies, deception, anger, inferiority, and – the biggest demon of all – insecurity. We will touch on this topic later on. I will break down these powerful, life-debilitating sources of pain and will give clear and concise reasons of why we hurt and why these root causes affect our daily lives. Many go from day to day living their lives as if the pain is non-existent. The pain is there and, unless it comes to the surface, we will always find that we are rejected, and abandoned and forgotten. Much, much worse: feeling inferior puts you in a corner, and that's not where you belong.

"You were made to shine my love, to glow, to prosper and be in health, even as your soul prospers." (NKJV –

Ephesians 3:20). You did not come into this world to be trampled on. You are meant to be loved and to love and to experience the fullness of that love and be rich in majestic splendor abiding and abounding in every situation. You were meant to go from glory to glory and spirit to spirit. You were meant to be a light in a dark world. Never again allow anything or anyone to tell you otherwise. I am here to tell you this, and much more, and to remind you every step of the way of this important fact, and that is: you are meant for greatness, darling.

So, let's explore together and make new paths and avenues to bring you closer, higher, and deeper into your destiny. You are meant to be loved, to love, and to contribute to a dying world because the best of you is coming forth. What's to come in your life, is coming forth, because this is your day, this is your hour, and it's not only your time, precious, it's your turn!

THE STARS ARE ALIGNING

You are reading this book because the stars aligned for you to pick up the book and read it. This is my love letter to you, my reader. When I say love letter, I do not use those words lightly and out of my mouth so easily. Love is not a word that should be thrown out loosely. Love is from God. Love is God. Love is you. Love is me. Love is your inner being. Love is the Universe. Love is amazing. We are all conduits of that amazing power called Love. I truly have a love for my reader to help the broken hearted, to help heal the wounds where mankind and forces of darkness have broken the lives of beautiful, sensitive, loving souls, who were meant to thrive and not be torn to shreds.

When you break someone's spirit, it is painful. It is hard to come back to yourself, lots of healing is needed. Picture a glass shattered on the floor. Ever try to put it back together? I don't think so – no, you threw it out. Who is then, qualified to teach and speak of this massive power called love ? I can tell you that I've walked in your shoes. Don't let anyone preach anything to you, unless they have walked in your shoes. We are the same size, girl; I have walked in your shoes. I have the credentials and they are being verbally abused, left out, forgotten, door slammed in my face. Yes, that qualifies me in the spiritual and natural realms. I am yes, appointed, anointed, and called of God, and the Universe to be the one to tell you that you will be set free, that you can live a happy life, free from bondage and fear.

I am an ordained evangelist, and Bible teacher, with years of counseling experience. I have taught the Bible for well over twenty years and have helped women hurting and at times couples, but I focused on women as that was my main ministry calling. I held outreaches in Long Island, New York, where thousands of people came weekly as I had guests from all over the country come and speak. I am a mother of three grown sons and that qualifies me as a nurturer. I am a woman of destiny, love, and power. Am I the one to be able to help someone? The answer is "Yes." God, I am certainly not perfect in my own right, but when I love, I am all in and I love deeply. Deep calling on to deep, as deep as the deepest oceans. I am alive and well today due to God's pure love for me. I also love to meditate, to grow daily in my meditations, and journal daily as well.

This is an interesting experience, when I say doors were shut in my face. It was back in Mexico with my love Richard. We were by the pool, I wanted to desperately go by the gazebo bar and get a piña colada drink. I shared that with my love, and he said, "I will go. You stay here." It was like a command. I said, "Can I come? There are swings, and we can take photos." He flipped out at the fact that I offered to go, and he took it wrong. He took it as if I was not trusting him to go to the bar alone, total misunderstanding. He really had no idea, I had visions of going on the swing and sipping on my piña colada. Well, that started a war. He said, "I am going to the pool. Don't come near me." Mind you, we are on vacation, my first time in Mexico.

I left him alone by the pool. I did not want to deal with him. I was not letting this man ruin my first day of the vacation. We walked back to the room, as he stepped in the hotel room, and I took a step in, he suddenly pushed the door on my face and locked me out of the hotel room. Now I am thinking well people are going to come out if I start yelling. Time passed and he finally opened the door. We discussed the situation about the pool, and we came to an understanding that we had a miscommunication. I was livid, so angry and emotions coming up and out of my mind. Someone else, would have banged the door down, cursed, screamed, but I did not have it in me. After being with Jeremy and now divorced from him, I just did not have it in me. I had no more fight in me. All I wanted was a piña colada.

These are experiences that have taught me to love myself. Experiences that I have come out of, and I know that I am the one called, appointed, and anointed with power from on high for such a time as this, to equip, empower, help align, and destroy the works of darkness that have afflicted your life. I will make sure to take the steps necessary to break the bondage that you have carried, and you will hear the birds chirp again. I can honestly tell you that life is a lesson learned daily in living and breathing. I have come out shining like gold, which goes through the fire. How is gold tried by fire? The gold must go through a trial by fire at a refinery. It is an exciting process called refining; it is re-liquified in a furnace of fire. Fire is a way to test gold, and when all the impurities are burned away, what's left is twenty-four karat gold – valuable indeed.

. Jeremy came home one evening, in another one of his lovely moods. He directly said to me, "You are uglier than Juanita." This statement came out of the blue. He could have been drinking. I said, "Well, I don't agree with you. I feel I am beautiful." He laughed and told me that he and his co-worker went to an eyeglass place to check out sunglasses and get an eye examination. He proceeded to tell me that he, and his friend from work, met a girl at the counter of an eyeglass place, and found her pretty. I said, "Yeah, where's she from?" He said, "She's Latina, black hair, brown eyes, sexy girl." I said, "Well, that was rude of you to say to me." For no rhyme or reason, he said those words to me, "You are uglier than Juanita."

I will never forget that deep indentation in my heart. The next day, well guess what, I wanted to see Juanita, and I drove myself to the eyeglass place to tell them I was looking for glasses, and I told them, my husband told me to ask for Juanita. The manager of the store introduced himself to me and said, "Juanita no longer works here. She was just transferred this morning to another location." He continued to tell me, "She was promoted to manager, and she is engaged to be married, and got her promotion and transfer, and she will now be living in another state." "Well, oh my," I said, "oh, wow, she was highly recommended." The manager answered, "She's terrific." Well, I never shared that I went there to Jeremy, but now pretty Juanita was no longer in the picture. The way Jeremy described her was as if they were going to hope to see her again.

Was it my insecurities that made me go there, or was it curiosity? Well, honestly, I think it was to see if I was uglier than her. I will never believe it. I am sure she was innocent, beautiful, sweet, and caring and Jeremy sure wished he had gotten to know her, but that door shut down in his face. I may not have handled this and other situations of rejection, abandonment, inferiority well, or like someone else, but I was running on rejection and curiosity.

When I first met Jeremy, it was love at first sight. He was loving, caring, and extremely charming. The one amazing thing about Jeremy, as I look back, that he had going for him, is he was an extremely good provider. As long as I was provided for financially, he kept on going with his life. It was as if he lived his life like a double-edged sword. I was fine being provided for and had all of my needs met. But I didn't have my husband. I was totally left alone and abandoned. It was sad as I knew he was a kind person, who truly loved God and people, but was not well, and his emotional state of being, was damaged even further when he found out he had heart issues. Of course, having all of those stents, and surgeries, and not being able to live a normal life made things even worse in our marriage. I tried so hard and for so long to hold on. Jeremy, I will always love you, for taking care of me and my family. It was unfortunate, our marriage turned, and we missed out on a beautiful life together. I truly believe he was not emotionally well.

THE EAGLE VERSUS THE CHICKEN

Eagle: Large soaring bird of prey noted for their size and strength in power of flight, belonging to the hawk family, with a massive wingspan, renowned for its sight and powerful soaring flight.

What is the spiritual meaning of the eagle?

The eagle spirit animal is associated with ambition, duty, fortitude, and willpower. They strive to achieve great heights and are rarely satisfied with anything less than the best that life has to offer.

What is the meaning of an eagle?

The eagle is the strongest and bravest of all birds. Eagles are courageous birds with extreme endurance and tenacity. Characteristics of an eagle are vision, fearless, tenacious, and high flyers. They never eat dead things or meat. They possess vitality, and nurture their young ones. They are known for their mastery, challenge, and independence. They take a broader view of the world and their place within it. They are naturally curious, as eagles love to learn and explore new ideas and master new skills and talents in pursuit of their goals. This is the personality of an eagle. Key facts about eagles are that they are the biggest birds of the planet. An eagle's eyesight is eight times better than the human's vision. There are more than sixty eagle species. They can see up to three kilometers away. They build their nests on top of high cliffs. They are a symbol of freedom and peace. Fun fact, bald eagles aren't bald. They have an incredible concentration. The eagle is called the "king of birds." The strongest bird is the world is the harpy eagle.

The moral of this eagle story is, "You become what you believe you are." For instance, are you a chicken or an eagle – which is the question.

Interesting thing about chickens: they can fly – it has been recorded that one flew for thirteen seconds. They can jump over fences, therefore, farmers cut their wings. They cannot keep flight due to their muscle weight and short wingspan, but they can fly a little bit. If you dream of becoming an eagle, follow your dreams, not the words of chickens. They are terrible flyers. Always remember, there are chickens everywhere, but eagles are rare. Eagles fly high to hunt at the top of the mountains, while chickens eat scraps of food in the yard. Eagles are strong and powerful, while chickens have been domesticated and are weaker and more fearful. You become what you believe you are.

In essence, we learned some excellent lessons from the eagle: to have strong vision and move with speed. Don't be like the chickens – be in the present, rise above the problems, find new opportunities out of your comfort zone, fly high, be courageous, and embrace the pain. The eagle thought he was a chicken, because he was an adopted eagle. The eagle's egg is placed in a chicken's nest and when it hatches the hen treats the eagle as a chicken and the eagle behaves as a chicken. Other chickens tell him he is an eagle, but he insists he is a chicken until one day he opens and spreads his wings and flies....

We need to have vision, willpower, remain focused, and never giving up in our lives. Eagles are silent. That is a good lesson to learn from the eagle: don't tell everything to everyone Not everyone is happy for you. Be fearless no matter what challenges you may face. Successful people are fearless. They face problems head on, no matter what size your problem is. Stay away from narrow-minded birds of prey, narrow-minded people. The people you hang around with will determine the person you become. Keep good company. Be tenacious, love the storms, get into the wind, and let it carry you and you will glide. Use the raging storms to lift you above the clouds. Eagles only flap their wings a few times, then they glide. Don't be anxious. Achievers are not afraid of challenges; they relish then and use them for profitability.

Don't rely on past failures or successes, however, rely on the now. Keep looking for new frontiers to conquer. Leave your past where it belongs – in the past. Eagles let their young ones fly. Let others fly, let them learn from you, and let them fly. Remarkably interesting thing, I find about eagles, that when the eagle grows old his feathers get stuck and old and they become weak and cannot take them as fast as it should in flight. This makes him weak and can make him die. He retires to a place far away in the mountains and while there he plucks out the weak feathers on his body and breaks his beak and his claws against the rocks until it is completely bare. Some have seen other eagles throw live animals down at the mulching eagle. This is a sad and bloody painful process. Then he stays in his hiding place until he has grown new feathers which takes about five months for the process. He begins to get a new beak and claws as well and then comes out flying higher than ever before. We need to also shed off the old, no matter how hard. Things that burden us and add no value to our lives should all be let go of.

Begin your new life, let go of the past, the wounds, and the hurts; learn from them as an experience that you will never allow again, and become an eagle. I am here explicitly to help you, I am here for you, to help you break free from the bondage of abuse, criticism, anger, inferiority, insecurity, identity crisis, fear, pain, and anguish. I am willing, and able, to break down these emotions and guide you into new place, a new height, and new purpose and new life. You deserve to love yourself again, find your identity, create a new world of joy and peace for yourself. Be willing to look deep into the crevices of your heart and begin a new chapter of your new life now. It takes drive, determination, willpower, and a whole lot of internal focus and preparation, so get ready to begin the healing process as we discover what broke you in the first place. The most beautiful thing is that you can love, and be loved again. This is my love letter to you.

At this juncture in my life, I have had much experience in counseling, and helping those who are dealing with emotional problems from breakups and divorces, as they deal with rejection, instability, separations, broken hearts, abandonment, verbal abuse, and identity crises. At this time of my life, my heart is open, ready, willing, and able to help as many people as I can. I work from home and give my time freely. I recall Margaret, as she was broken down, with the shock of infidelity, and Celine, as well, lost with nowhere to go after her life came crashing down after divorce. I have steps laid out in this book, which will enable you to follow, and I am always available, to help set short-term and long-term goals with you, my reader, if ever needed.

I have walked in your shoes. I have been in break-ups, divorced, abandoned, rejected, made fun of, belittled, and have had emotions that could have broken me to the core. I know how you feel when you say you hurt. I know what it's like to feel alone, like no one is listening. I know what it's like when others ignore you, and don't even care. I have been there. You crawl into your space and survive in the pain. I believe I am here for such a time as this, to help those with broken hearts, broken lives, and pain you cannot even describe. My desire is to grow in my evangelism, counseling, life coaching career, and help you decipher and explore, and dig into the crevices, which hold you back from becoming the best that you can be. You got this, and you are not alone.

I am elated at where I am in my life, and I look forward to helping as many people as I possibly can. My experiences, and counseling experiences, have got me to this point, of writing this book, and my heart is open and receptive to help as many people as I possibly can, as I have grown and reached new heights in building my career. I am elated for growth, that I know I can help others going through similar situations, of breakups and divorces, and even loss, as I have experienced. I have come a long way even in the past year, I have grown tremendously in my outlook on life, my positive thinking, my prayer life, my meditations, my daily journaling. I have created a wholesome, safe environment for myself, but it takes choice, a choice to want to be whole, to want to be emotionally healed of all the baggage that we have carried throughout the years and relationships we have encountered. I can say, I am at a stage in my life, in which by becoming a life coach, and also having the experience as a traveling evangelist, and counselor, that I have helped others come to a place in their lives that they can find the freedom, purpose, and visions for their lives. I am fully emotionally strong, ready, willing, and able to give a helping hand to those that need and desire to live fulfilled lives, letting go of the past, and moving and surging on to what's ahead, a newfound life of love, peace, joy, freedom, and purpose.

"But He knows the way that I take; when He has tested me, I shall come forth as gold."

— JOB 23:10, NKJV

ON EAGLES' WINGS

Alone again, I lost my friend,
In Eagles' eyes, you were my skies
We flew together, like birds of a feather,
You were my cover, my wonderful lover
As days go by, I look to fly,
Strong in my dive, like an eagle in the sky
Alone again, I'm getting strong,
Memories of you, will still belong
Like an eagle in the sky, I glide, I soar,
As oceans roar, with you, no more.

— MYRNA IVETTE CLAUDIO

3

THE WORLD IS YOUR OYSTER

Yes, the world is your oyster: the world is there for the taking. The reason we live lives, hidden in our emotional damaged existence, is because we have not allowed the inner-being to show us the love and affection, and worthiness we own as human beings. God, the Universe, and your inner-being are all in sync working together to bring us the best of the best, in our lives. We have been trained to the best of our abilities, but there is more, so much more to be discovered, and it's found inside of our inner-being. It is your instinct, your inner GPS, your guide, your source, your intuition. You have learned many things in your lives. But the answer to your questions in life reside inside of you. It is the gift of yourself, your inner-being. As you learn, within the pages of this book, you will get a glimpse of ways of finding who you truly are and were always meant to be, your true north, the love for yourself, and your being. My heart and soul are excited to share what I have found, and how I found myself, and how I found my identity back.

MARGARET HENDERSSON'S STORY

I met Margaret through a friend; she became my client, and soon thereafter, a beautiful friend. Margaret needed counseling because of the situation she experienced with her husband. As we were sitting, we are enjoying a cup of coffee, as she begins to cry quietly. She said, "I've told no one." I tried to console her and asked her to take a few deep breaths, as she then told me that her husband started a relationship with another woman, and Margaret was numb and in total shock. I asked her if he shared this information with him, she said no, someone called and told her, that worked in the same office. Her heart was broken.

At this time, she had a five year old daughter and she felt like the world had collided on top of her. The only words out of her mouth are, "Please pray, just pray. I don't want to talk. I just need prayer." I told her I would certainly do that for her. She was so distraught; she didn't even stay to talk. She was so overwhelmed. She was dealing with so many feelings of rejection, confusion, betrayal. I asked her if she could reschedule for the following Friday to talk, and she agreed. Amazingly enough, she came Friday to her appointment and told me she confronted him, and he admitted to her, and he told her that he would break it up with this girl. He said he loved her and made a mistake. Margaret told him she was packing to leave that weekend. He begged her not to go, but she did.

They were separated for more than eight months, and I continued to see her for counseling. In one of her sessions with me, she shared that, out of anger, she went to a party, met a guy, and they made out. She said that was it, but that she did it out of spite. She cried again, and I share with her some steps to face the broken emotions she was facing. I worked with her and I was asking her what are you feeling inside, she told me she loved her husband and wanted him back and that she was miserable without him. She shared that he had been going to see a counselor himself, and that he wanted to work out their marriage. He broke it off with the girl, and immediately got into counseling. She said, "That is my husband, and I will be back with him, I know it, and I believe it, and no one can tell me differently." I am amazed at her tenacity. At this point in the counseling, she had been following the steps that I had given her to do, such as daily journaling, setting short and long term goals, meditation, positive affirmations, and written assignments. She was working through her emotions as well as I continued to work things through with her.

Weeks later she calls him, and she shared with me that he had broken up with the girl he was seeing that he wanted them to go to marriage counseling together, and that he could not live without her. I did not hear from her for a long while but, a year later, they had a son. To this day, they live happily, and they both did follow through with the marriage counseling for a long while. They now enjoy each other, have three beautiful children.

What is the moral of this story? Perhaps not every relationship ends in breakups, and yet they suffered an infidelity situation. Margaret said to me, that it was her belief in God, strong Catholic upbringing, that brought them back together. She thanked me for all of the counseling and work I gave her, especially bringing emotions to the surface, and allowing her damaged emotions to rise up to the surface to be exposed and healed. She told me it was her faith, and although she tried to be with another man, it wasn't the man she loved.

In her counseling sessions, she truly worked on the homework I gave her, and she worked on steps to healing, forgiveness, and wellness that I prepared for her. She started the goal setting, meditation, and positive affirmations; this all made her feel like a brand-new woman. It makes me so happy to know they both worked at it, and pursued to stay together in their family, as forgiveness and true love was the superior thing in their marriage.

Thank you, Margaret, for being my friend and I am so happy for both of you. You have a beautiful marriage, and blessed children and family. God bless you all.

I find that in Margaret's case, the love superseded all of the outside forces, which came to break up their marriage. They felt strongly enough about each other, and both truly wanted to be together and raise their family. Forgiveness here was the key action that they both so bountifully gave each other. Some people do not ever accept or condone infidelity. We cannot judge how another person will react in a situation like this, as in Margaret's case, forgiveness won, and they restored their marriage to wholeness via the conduit of love.

THE PROCESS HERE WITHIN

In the pages of this book, I will break down insecurities and identity crisis, as you will gain knowledge of the type of wounds and hurts that have created pain such as rejection, anger, insecurities, abandonment, fears, and verbal abuse, and will take the steps necessary to work on your healing process. I break down insecurities, and we find out the root causes. For instance, in my case, with my mom working when I was a little child, I was raised by my grandmother, and I lacked that closeness with my mom in my younger years, causing deep insecurities. That is a root cause. Another fear from my past, in my relationships, I had difficulty, even with breakups, or being left alone, so I would stay in relationships that were not so good for me. Break down the demon of insecurity as the root emotion of all emotions, because when you are insecure, you can trigger a fear of being alone. It also causes jealousy. In this lifetime, people have even committed murder due to insecurities and jealousy; many movies have come out due to this subject. It is important we deal with and break down the root causes of insecurity. In these pages we extensively break down the emotion of insecurity and its root causes.

In these pages, we will discuss fear and rejection. At this juncture, you will learn to take the steps necessary to gain control of your new life by framing your outcome and learning to take time for yourself, taking walks, car rides, beach, travel, socializing, self-gratification, self-love, practicing meditation, prayer, journaling daily, positive affirmations in order to begin your inner healing, and taking the steps to clearing the path to a more fulfilling and beautiful life. We break down the subject of abuse, verbal-abuse, rejection complex, fear issues, and healing of damaged emotions. In these pages, we discuss the emotion of rejection and fears and how to heal from these emotions.

As kings and queens, we wear our crowns, maybe they're off to the side a little bit, but we are royalty. You will know who you are, and what you want out of life, and you will know your self-worth. You will go from a caterpillar to a butterfly, as the transformation has now begun to take place. It is imperative to stay away from negative people and influences. We learn what is in the mirror, what we see, and want to be. We begin practicing the seed of a new thing, called positive affirmations, making deposits into our spirit beings. We journal daily. It's time to straighten our crowns.

Never give up and never give in. We will learn the reasons not to allow any past wounds or insecurities to steal our joy, we will learn how far we have come. Here we let our yes be yes and our no be no. How important it is to take the steps to finding time for you. How it's going to take faith and believing in order to achieve the mark of the high calling of your life.

Last but not least, in these pages, you will find a great love awakening to realize, that this is not just your time, but it's your turn. You will gain a new understanding of the benefits and practices of what you have learned here and achieved, in order to now begin your new bright, successful future and create a new life for yourself. We discuss the love of self, your north star, how we can love again, and my love letter to you, my reader. Know, it's not just your time, but it is your turn. You are next in line for a new and miraculous life, which awaits you in the reading of these pages.

ABUSE AND ITS CAUSES

Being abused comes in so many forms. Abuse is a treatment of cruelty or violence, even once, regularly, or repeatedly. Abuse is when someone causes us harm or distress. It can take many forms, ranging from disrespect to causing someone physical or mental pain. It can occur in someone's home, a care home, a hospital, or a public place. Often the people who commit abuse are taking advantage of a special relationship. It causes deep hurt and anguish. It is so important that you speak to someone if you are experiencing any type of abuse from anyone.

WORDS CUT DEEP

Words are cutting and painful in an abusive situation. This is quite interesting: what the Bible says about the tongue.

> *"But no man can tame the tongue. It is unruly evil, full of deadly poison."*
>
> —JAMES 3:8, NKJV

With the tongue, you can speak sweet nothings into someone's ear, you can sing melodies of love, you can profess your love to your bride or lover, and with the same tongue, you can stab someone in the back, and use words that cut so deep that the hearer would have to go through much healing or at least reflect on such deep wounds and pain. What is a tongue? Your tongue is a muscle and, as a muscle, can be powerful in good and in bad situations.

I love to use my tongue to make positive affirmations daily, which I will describe in more detail in another chapter. Positive affirmations help us in affirming who we are, what we are, and where we are going. You use the same positive affirmations daily or you can change them up. You can even sing them as you drive or take a nice walk. Positive affirmations are positive phrases and statements that are repeated to help challenge negative thoughts and encourage positive changes in your life. Let me tell you, when I say those positive affirmations daily, or even change them up, I mean them, I believe what am saying. I am not just throwing words out in the air just for the heck of it – no, I am affirming to the Universe, within my inner being, that what I am saying is true and it's yes and amen. I truly, with every inch of my being, believe what I am saying. Now, going back to Margaret ,do you remember what she said? She said, "That is my husband, and I will be back with him, I know it and I believe it, and no one can tell me differently."

She said it aloud, she confessed it with her heart, she believed it, her inner woman knew her man, she knew her person, she knew her future. Margaret was not just crying out for help.

In this book, you will discover how to find emotional stability, how to heal from heartache and pain, how to put your broken pieces together, how to forgive the unforgivable, how to be free of anger and resentment, how to feel whole, happy and secure again, how to regain your identity that was stolen by deceivers, how to find your inner peace, how to learn to love again, and love yourself even more, how to learn to love life and be social again, and how to learn to live your best life now.

One of the ways is positive affirmations as Margaret used. She learned how to put the broken pieces together, and forgive the unforgivable. There are other methods of course that you may already use: prayer, meditation, daily journaling, forgiving. There are many avenues. Some use yoga, some love taking walks or long drives. Meditation can give you a sense of calm, peace, and balance, as you take nice deep breaths. This can benefit your emotional wellbeing and your overall health. You can also use it to relax and cope with stress. It helps you stay balanced and centered. There are many facets of meditation. I like to meditate fifteen to thirty minutes daily. It allows me to bring focus to my daily life. It can certainly be a wonderful tool to use as you are healing from a breakup and dealing with a broken heart and damaged emotions.

WHAT IS LOVE ANYWAY?

I want to go to a subject that is world renowned. That is the subject spoken of usually prior to a relationship going downhill. It is the massive and powerful word called "love."

Like the song, what's love got to do, got to do with it? (Tina Turner)

Love is like a fantasy bubble, a truth, a great feeling that's so amazing you can die, a feeling of bliss, a lifetime event, or a moment in time. Love is a tale, a lie, maybe in this life we'll find out. Some may have found love, real love, or have experienced it in one form or another, even if they believe it was for a moment in time. To some, love is now gone, vanished by the winds of time, or stolen by the other woman, or the other man, who knows. Some may have shattered lives, brokenness, divorce, or even been thrown out of places, or abandoned, and they called it love.

Deceived by lying dogs, some are using this word to get you to spend time with them for passion, lust, and greed, as they abuse human hearts and souls scattered all over this earth. Oh, the best of all, to all who are seeking this love, or have found it, is it real, or is it fake.? Before you use those three little powerful words, "I love you," and use them so loosely, think again: it can devastate a human heart to the point of sickness, disease, suicide, heartbreak, and deep suffering. *Love* is not a feeling, *love* is a commitment. *Love* is a dedicated state of mind that two humans enter into, some knowing and some not knowing, the power of this massive word called love. Feelings come and go, people come and go, and times change, people change, but hear this, when you know love, real love, not the imposter of love, when you know *love*, it is born of *integrity*. The one thing I do know is love is God and God is love.

"Beloved, let us love one another, for love is of God, and everyone who loves is born of God and knows God."

—1 JOHN 4:7, NKJV

Humanity in its natural realm, could not comprehend the power of this massive entity called *love*.

It is written in the stars, it is kind, passionate, giving, and mostly it is a commitment that is not hard to keep when you love and adore someone so much, that even after years of knowing each other you still get those butterflies that you got the first time you met. The spiritual meaning of butterflies is that they are not only beautiful they have mystery, and are a metaphor representing spiritual rebirth, transformation, change, hope, and life. In Margaret's case, she experienced a mystery of faith and positive affirmations, she discovered the meaning of rebirth in her marriage and the vows to her husband. Margaret discovered change, hope, and a new life. Like a butterfly, her love had a transformation. Butterflies symbolize the metamorphosis from the common, colorless caterpillar to the exquisite, winged creature of delicate beauty, the butterfly has become – as I mentioned, transformation and hope. Across many cultures, it has become a symbol of rebirth and resurrection. As you see, Margaret experienced a resurrected new life, new hope, and a new marriage. It is also a symbol of triumph of the spirit and the soul over the physical person. This incredible colorless caterpillar transforms to beauty. In essence, many of us are familiar with the phrase beauty from ashes, it is a comeback from loss, of a phoenix rising from destruction, finding the good in the midst of the ugly.

You can break free from the tendencies of abuse and fear. You can get your identity and self-worth back. Breakups and divorce, even if temporary, can be painful. This book offers a compassionate and spiritual path, in which you will see yourself in the pages of this book transform your emotions that you may have encountered and that are broken down such as:

- Insecurity
- Fear
- Anger
- Abandonment
- Loss of Identity (Identity Crisis)
- Inferiority
- Rejection
- Light

We need to see the light, we need a transformation, a revolution in the spirit realm. Light is one of the most universal and fundamental symbols. It is the spiritual and the divine, it is illumination and intelligence. Light is the source of goodness and the divine. Light is one of the things that I pray for when I wake up in the morning; I want to turn the light on, so I can see. In some apartments in New York City, when you turn the lights on, the roaches scatter. The light drives away the bad and the ugly and light exposes all evil. That is why the term is used: it will all come to light. Light is a gift. It is something beautiful like the sun shining during the day and light of the moon at night. The light also comes from the stars that twinkle on a clear night.

In the Bible, or in the spiritual realm of things, light has been a symbol of holiness, goodness, knowledge, wisdom, grace, hope, and God's revelation. In contrast, darkness has been also known to be associated at times with despair. I want light in my life, transparency, and truth. I do not want to live my life in a dark corner, or in any kind of darkness. Love, light, peace, and joy are beautiful attributes that will come to all who seek to want to conquer that light. My desire is for you to be free and may the light shine in any dark places that have kept you bound in the secret places of darkness that some may not even know about, but once free, you will never look back.

In the pages of this book, you will discover the meaning of these emotional distresses and baggage you do not need to carry around with you. You can find healing in your hurt and brokenness and create a new life of hope, love, and pure bliss and joy. You can find stability and peace as you experience new avenues and paths to a new light to finding self-love and restoration. A new you is on the horizon. Get excited and have hope, vision, as you will find your voice and a new life waiting for you.

FLY, BUTTERFLY, FLY

As the caterpillar goes through its metamorphosis, so will you; stand strong, never give up and never give in. Keep your vibrations high, stay centered, keep loving, and you will enjoy a light that has no words, a flame that sparkles back and forth, as the light glistens and shines in and out of you throughout the many beautiful days you have to come. Most importantly, be you, be free, be authentic, never be a yes person – unless you want to say yes – yes people are a dime a dozen – always be keen, aware, awakened to the now, and to the knowledge that you were created as a masterpiece in this Universe to do great and mighty works. You are called for such a time as this to be a carrier of the glory, to be set apart, to be different without giving, and owing no human any explanation. Be so free, that you only care about what is taught to you as right and wrong in your mindset. People go around telling people, "You are out of your mind." I say, "No, buddy I am out of your mind." Have your mind, make wise decisions, live your life to the fullest. Yesterday is gone, you cannot bring it back, tomorrow is not promised to you, my friend, but you do have now, this moment, this amazing moment in time, which is the key to your destiny. Take a deep breath, right now: inhale, now exhale. Now, today, is all you are promised, my dear loved one.

Take life by the horns and run with it. Make changes, buy the dress, take the trip, make new friends, remove the bad ones, dance in the rain, make the video, write the book, make the movie, be that which you are called to be because I promise you, that yesterday is gone and was, and had been; remember that now all you have about yesterday is a memory. Tomorrow, I promise you, no one has promised you. You have *now*, this second, this time in space, in the Universe and galaxies and stars to shine your light like never before. Shout on the rooftop, be free – you are one amazing person. Get real with your life. Stop procrastinating. Time was written for you before the beginning of time came into being. You need to catch up with yourself, and meet the dreams and desires at the point of contact. Don't allow the demons of anger, fear, inferiority, insecurity, and the like to hinder your walk. You can stay in a clear and strong path, but it is an ugly and miserable path to stay where you are. It is time to stop lurking to see who will hurt you next.

Whose victim you will be a target of next because, I promise you, you will fall prey again to another liar, another cheater, another gossiper, another breakup, another backbiter. It's time to take the steps necessary to change and change now. My heart's desire is that you take these words in this book and become an eagle and be a free butterfly, no longer a victim of hurt and pain. You can heal, you can break free, you can have all your dreams come true and much more. Just do it.

"Therefore if the son makes you free, you shall be free indeed."

— JOHN 8:36, NKJV

BE FREE MY LOVE

Be free my love,
Do not be sad
For I am with you,
So please be glad
My love is yours,
Forever more
I will never leave you,
That's what's in store
So be secure,
My maiden love
For I am with you,
And that's for sure
Be free to fly,
The skies above
The sky's limit,
I am your love!

— MYRNA IVETTE
CLAUDIO

4

INSECURITY AND IDENTITY CRISIS

It is rather important to understand the steps you need to take in order to get rid of the damage that we have experienced with emotional distresses. It is imperative to get to know the intensity and meaning behind these emotions that can cause insecurity and identity crisis in our lives. I will go in depth in the meanings of key damaged emotions. Gaining this knowledge is key to gaining your freedom. We want to get to the point that even when healed, and these emotions pop up, we know their name, and root causes. These key emotional wounds create deep pain within us, causing us to shut down, and to not see clearly the path to which we are called to take. To name a few we will be discussing, they are rejection, insecurity, anger, abandonment, fear, verbal abuse, identify crisis, and lack of self-worth. You must get to a place where you, the reader, understand all of these emotions, which will be broken down, and know their differences. The purpose is the get to the root causes and become set free, and live fruitful, eventful, and secure lives.

I have dealt with the issues of insecurity since I was a little girl. As far as I can remember, I have felt insecure in many areas of my life. I come from a stable, loving family. My mom and dad worked all their lives to make sure us three girls had the best of everything. Maybe, I felt they're not being home all the time as an internal loss. I spent a lot of time with my grandmother, God rest her soul, Mami Purin, and it was so beautiful to be around her. I felt like a gold treasure that she found. She loved me like her daughter, gave me baths, took me to school, and even took me to New York City to see the World's Fair. I was on a plane to New York. It was my first time. I have no remembrance of mom raising me, because she worked, and although she was successful at her job, I missed being with my mom. That could have given me unknown feelings of insecurity, maybe and maybe not, and my grandma filled my mother's shoes so gracefully. As I grew up, my relationship to my mom flourished when they decided to come to New York to live from Puerto Rico. I must have been seven or eight years old when I finally became closer to my mother and got to know her better.

I shared with you earlier, about the bride wifey in the honeymoon, on the boat, when she put me down for being Puerto Rican, and not having a beautiful satin dress like hers. I have come such a long way from that honeymoon young girl. But it did cost me a pretty penny of suffering, and a long list of damaged emotions and insecurities that I never shared with anyone. It in turn, hurt my relationships, and I had relationship issues in my past, such as being so insecure, I would feel left and abandoned a few times for other women. I was not healed. I truly felt like a broken bird, with a broken leg crossing a crowded street, waiting for a truck to hit me on the other side. That was my mentality. Crazy enough, the truth is, that the better the relationship was, the worse I felt. I felt as if a ball would come from left field. It was certainly not that I wasn't in love with my partner, but that I was always looking behind me for the next shoe to drop. That is a horrible way to live. It's called insecurity. I had it, and due to that debilitating emotion, I experienced inferiority and abandonment issues.

It certainly did not help when in one of my relationships, every small argument or dumb fight, he would say, "I'm leaving. I am done." I kept saying to him, "How is that going to help me ever heal if you say you love me but keep throwing in my face that you are leaving?" I knew he loved me. He was causing more insecurities, and fears of being alone, fears of being abandoned. "Who am I? Why shouldn't I just let him go, and I can be a free woman?" most normal women would say. But no, not me, I would say things like, "Sit down. Let's talk. You love me, you said you did, that is the wrong way to go about this." He would profess his love and say, "It's your insecurities," as he would talk with me. I learned to let time pass maybe a few hours, cooling time, after he would get upset, to just let time pass, and after a few hours, we would talk it through. I have come a long way since then and have healed and learned who I am as a human being. I am worth it; I am secure, and I am free from that spirit of timidity.

I always found in my relationships that when someone hurts you, we always must keep in mind that hurt people, hurt people. One of the chapters of this book will discuss in detail setting yourself free by forgiving. Many books have been written on this subject; I sense my spiritual outlook on it may come from a different angle. The most amazing thing about being set free – which is the goal, after you finish and take steps necessary after you read this book – is that it never is the person who is hurting you, but that truly it is causing all the issues to rise up, in our lives. The reason we keep hurting is we keep going in circles, like a dog after his tail, with the same rejection issues, the same jealousy issues, the same abandonment feeling. They are real, and yes, painful.

I know they were caused at an onset in your life. Maybe we can find out when? That would be interesting. However, the point I am trying to make is that once you see the cycle of broken relationships, or effects of that, such as damaged emotions, that's when we need to examine it, and why this cycle continues to happen in our life. What is happening that I am always feeling inferior, and insecure, and rejected? Believe me, there are paths to take to avoid each and every one of those effects that have hindered your life for years. Let's get free, let's get real, let's get raw. It may be a little painful for a while, but after a while, you will come out like gold in the fire. You will know who you are, and whose you are, and where you are going, and have many answers to questions, you didn't even know you thought you had. Let's explore and with the help of God, the Universe or your precious inner being, let us examine the root causes that have hindered your life, and be set free once and for all.

QUESTIONS YOU MAY ENCOUNTER AFTER A BREAKUP

This chapter breaks down how I came to see the light in a dark and fearful world. Below are the effects of relationships ending, which are broken down here.

- How do I gain my self-worth back
- How do I find my identity back
- How can I be secure again
- How do I heal from rejection, abandonment, rejection, and verbal abuse
- How do I deal with the pain of grieving
- How do I stop my anger, frustration, and fears
- How do I forgive
- How do I gain my self-respect back

- How do I sleep normally again
- Fear of being alone
- Where would I live
- How would I raise my children alone

EFFECTS OF INSECURITY

In this chapter, we are going to concentrate on the biggest demon of all: insecurity. Call it that because it hides and acts like a sweet little emotional thing. It's called insecurity and it is uncertainty or anxiety about oneself, and lack of confidence. Its effect is a feeling of inadequacy, of not being good enough, and uncertainty. It produces anxiety about your goals, relationships, and the ability to handle certain situations that arise from day to day.

Everyone deals with some kind of insecurity from time to time. It can affect areas of our lives and come from a variety of causes. A common example of feeling insecure is jealousy in a relationship. That was an effect that I had and that made me feel like I needed to always control the situations. Another is being jealous of others instead of rejoicing in their achievements. You can also get irritated by the way someone acts, feelings of self-doubt, procrastination on some difficult tasks, worried about things on a regular basis. There are also insecure people that adapt shyness and uncertainty about others. At times they feel their mate is cheating and are constantly worried about being abandoned. It is important to note that insecurity could stem from a traumatic event, such as a divorce, a breakup, a loss, or abuse, be it physical or verbal abuse.

CONSTRUCTIVE WAYS TO HELP SOMEONE OR A FRIEND WHO SUFFERS FROM INSECURITY

- Don't tell them they're wrong

- Ask if they want to talk and share how they feel
- Reassure them constructively
- Affirm their value, let them know you are there

STEPS TO HEALING FROM INSECURITIES

- Prioritize your needs
- Be mindful
- Speak highly of yourself
- Do positive affirmations
- Embrace the awkward feelings
- Examine and challenge your thoughts
- Meditation (fifteen to thirty minutes daily)
- Journal your thoughts daily – start writing
- Reflect on the good
- Talk about it to someone you know will hear you
- Accept what you can't control
- Focus on the present moment
- Live by your core values
- Keep good company
- Listen to music or do a happy dance
- Take walks, or go for a drive
- Be around people who share your values and socialize with them
- Tidy up, organize your home as your sanctuary
- Take action of what matters
- Get good sleep
- Eat healthy take good care of your body
- Exercise
- Drink water
- Believe in yourself

Insecure people need to become conscious of the emotions they encounter, so they know what they are dealing with, and so they can change them. The reason this chapter is centered on insecurity when we have other topics of emotional healing is that I believe it's the most deceiving, the quietest, the little mouse, but yet the elephant in the room. Insecurity is the mama bear of all the other emotions because when you are insecure you then feel inferior, you feel abandoned, you get fear, you get rejection issues. It is such a big demon of all demons, that I call it that because it's the little one hiding in the corner. How do you think best seller books are written and Oscar winning movies are made? They stem from someone who was insecure feeling a condition lower in status than others. Feeling lesser, lower in rank, position, quality, and power.

Mama bear *insecurity* is oh, so shy, so quiet, oh, I am just so insecure. Everybody's feeling bad for her. Oh, I just feel so bad for that emotion – no, I don't, because I have had enough experience to know this is the biggest spirit of damaged emotions of all and why? Insecurity will cause a person who is damaged to hurt another human being. Follow me as I travel with this insecure emotion; it is insecure, then it gets mad, causes anger, then gets jealous, and jealousy can lead to fighting, jealousy can lead to murder. Yes, murder all because of the little hidden cause and effect of an insecure person. If you write all the damaged emotions, you can trickle it down to it being the mama bear. No one sees it like that, but it is the root cause.

Many have written murder mysteries, and filmed movies where a lover gets killed because the other lover found out there was infidelity. It all began with jealousy, envy, fear, and why? Because of an insecure human being. I am not fooled by this emotion, at all, it certainly does not belong in the human existence. It is my calling to call you out. I am not fooled. It is in your power to examine these steps above that I have laid out and will break down in the next chapter.

It is important to make certain that the human heart is

always treated with the utmost respect in the process of healing its emotions. I will break down emotions such as abandonment, fear, unforgiveness, and rejection's root causes. I call them root causes because they have created a root in your being that needs to be uprooted, not in the natural sense of the word, but in the inner person, in the inner woman, in the inner man.

Those root causes have gripped in your heart, they live there, and some live in your mindset. They need to be uprooted and damaged emotions need to be healed so once and for all you are not getting angry for every little thing or having any fears and doubts that creep up at times for no reason at all. Did you ever just get upset and you don't even know why? It is because there is a damaged emotion that is rooted in you from verbal abuse, a broken relationship, a death, a divorce, or even abuse from a past relationship or as a child at home or at school. Let's get free. Let's live a life without roots that hold us back from being who we were created and meant to be.

A secure person is confident, easygoing, levelheaded, poised, relaxed, self-assured, serene, tranquil, unruffled (I like this one the best), assured, courageous, calm, cool. It is respect for oneself and one's position. Those are the attributes I desire in my life.

THE TRAUMA OF EXPERIENCING IDENTITY CRISIS

Identity crisis (noun) – a period of uncertainty and confusion in which a person's sense of identity becomes insecure, typically due to a change in their expected aims or role in society. the definition of (the noun) identity crisis does, in fact, mention the word insecure. This is exactly what I am getting at when I say *insecurity* is the main head of the household of damaged emotions. When you don't know who you truly are, you will identify as having an identity crisis, and I don't mean this in the sense of the natural realm of life. I am talking more in the spiritual sense. In the Spirit, when we feel that confusion after a breakup situation, we feel a sense of loss, of not being able to be ourselves, for even awhile. It happens to people that have lost loved ones. They get this sense of loss, of not coping the way that they used to cope prior to losing their loved one. Identity is your mark, it is who you are, it is your personal wellbeing. When you feel the loss of a loved one, a divorce, a broken relationship, an abusive situation, you can go through steps of feeling as if your identity is not so much gone, but you may sense a loss of you, a loss of who you were yesterday, when you went to work, or for a drive. It can be for a brief moment, or a brief few weeks – sometimes the loss and confusion can last longer. These are raw emotions we are dealing with, and so sensitive.

When you have an attachment to another human being it causes a soul tie – two souls to tie together in love and harmony – but when that breaks, you feel like you have lost your world, like you cannot function right, or even sleep or eat. At times, no one understands how you really feel. Your identity with this person, or your pain, of verbal abuse went so deep that you feel that you are not even yourself anymore. You feel lost, forgotten, and like a bird, retreat to the little branch on the tree. Identity crisis is an emotional state of mind, that sometimes takes time to heal. Broken pieces have got to come back together, and it takes time to heal. You say to yourself, "Who am I? Why am going through this? What is going on?" That is deep pain and going through this identity crisis. It is real and must be given its proper time to heal.

There are certain things that take time to heal, such as grief, divorce, and even broken relationships. There is the gift of time, for a wounded soul. I believe that as I write my experiences and lay out simple steps, there will be a process of time and love that needs to be poured out. It's like a garden of vegetables: you have to water it, tend to it, and see it grow. The most important aspect here is having a heart that is pliable, a heart of flesh. There are people with stony hearts, who will go through life, and never get healed, and live life angry and suffering, ending up sick because they do not take care of their bodies. It is just as important to take care of your outer body as it is to take care of your inner soul. A man with gangrene in his foot, who does not get help, will lose the foot. That's a deep analogy but true; if you do not take care of your garden, your fruit will just not grow. You will not grow and be the person you were created to be if you do not have the pliable heart, but instead a stony heart. What happens when you plant a seed on cement? It will not grow, it will not flourish. Seeds of love and healing need to be planted with a heart that is ready, soft, and willing and able to be open to change and want to create a new life for yourself. Most importantly, be real, and be true to yourself. You were created for such a time as this.

There are other root causes of pain and hurt which come from, as you know already, insecurity, others being inferiority, fear, rejection, anger, resentment, anguish, abandonment, unforgiveness. These are the classic causes of damaged emotions when you experience a hard break up, or another life-changing event.

"The Lord is close to the brokenhearted; He rescues those whose spirits are crushed."

— PSALMS 34:18, NLT

YOUR INNER BEING

Inner peace comes with a price,
That you paid for
All of your life
I am here to bring you peace,
I am your inner voice
So please be still,
And make no noise
I abide in you,
I'm always here
So be at peace,
And do not fear
Take the time,
To know me well
I live inside you,
As you can tell
I wait for you, into the night
For you to come, and be alright
I'm always here
I live so near!

— MYRNA IVETTE
CLAUDIO

5

GROWING LOVE PAINS

The time has come to frame your world, and become direct, focused, and ready for the preparation of the steps we are taking. I am not just talking about literal steps, but also, spiritual steps, steps in your heart, steps in your mind. We want to frame your outcome to deliberately, and determined to become the new you, the you who knows yourself. Some of these steps could be a simple as taking a walk, taking a drive, just doing something for you in a rewarding self-gratification stance. It takes practice to do something as a habit.

For instance, as your day begins, and you make a list of things to do, and do them. Habit is what brings results. Habit is continual action, without giving up. Once you see the result, that is satisfying to a person. Changes in our lives unfortunately, don't come easy, and they take habit and work; it's called growing love pains. It is so key to place yourself at the top of the list, and although you may have little ones, and they do need care, of course, don't forget *you*. Without you being whole and strong, it will be harder to take care of them. I look at it this way, but this is me, I am the queen of my castle, the queen of my kingdom, and I matter. You matter very much. Take good care of yourself – put yourself first – all else will follow only according to your kingdom rules. You reign, you rule, you are mighty, you are awesome.

ROXY'S STORY

Roxy, at the time, was twenty-nine years old. This happened after she started getting sober. She realized why she was getting so high; she was filling an empty hole that never got filled when she was growing up. She went to AA meetings, twice a day or at least one time a day for twenty-one years. She met someone in AA, as they conversed, he told her he was an orphan at eight years old and lived in Colorado. He did not have a mother or father. She was soon to find out he was a pathological liar. When they were about to get married, she found out he had a mother in Phoenix, Arizona, and that his parents were divorced, and his father was the Assistant Dean of Business, in the university of Arizona. Roxy also found out he had four siblings, who all went to graduate school, and they were all well established. Roxy did not know this until later. She started finding out that he was a compulsive liar. He went to a special school for children with conduct disorder issues. He ran away at fifteen years old. He ended up living with an older gay man. He may have been abused at the school.

Roxy's parents bought a house for them, and Roxy's husband, Dylan, started working for Roxy's father. Things seemed perfect to Roxy, but piece by piece, she started finding out some truths. She then became pregnant with her first child, and it was wonderful. Dylan was not home much because he was going to school for work in Vermont. Roxy was suspicious all this time, because she suspected that he was having affairs with other women, which of course, he denied. This is when Dylan started to become physically abusive. Dylan just kept punching the wall right beside her head. This really scaring the daylights out of her. He would punch the dashboard of their car, and wrecked it. Roxy was so upset as this was their family vehicle. He would throw objects around the home, he became abusively worse.

Dylan decided he wanted to work on his own and left the family business. This is when Dylan was in charge of depositing money in the bank, but never did. There were signs out on the register of the supermarket not to accept any checks from Dylan and Roxy Brown. Roxy knew at this time, that she wanted to get out of the marriage, however, Roxy wanted to have one more child. Plus, it was hard for her, to say anything like, "I want to get out of the marriage," as her husband would get violent, and was a compulsive liar, if anything was brought up. She hung in there for a little while longer and had her second child.

Roxy now had two little ones, and Dylan was working on his own, and God knows what he was doing with the money. If Roxy had five dollars for every time he came home at three in the morning, she would have been a millionairess. Throughout all this, Dylan was in the program. When he would go to a meeting and never come home at a reasonable hour, Roxy would call one of his sponsors, who would tell her that he never even showed up at the meeting. Now, Roxy really knew that she had to get out. One night her husband called and said that he was attacked, and that someone threw dirt in his face, and he must have swallowed pebbles, and he had to go to the emergency room. What Roxy found was that he swallowed the screen from a cracked pipe, and yet he still denied that he was doing anything. When Dylan returned from his escapade, he went back to work, he was walking up to the front door, and Roxy walked out to meet him. That is when he told Roxy he was smoking crack. Roxy proceeded to punch him in the face, told him to call his sponsor and to get out of the house. He left the house, went to rehab, and she told him he could not come to visit his children, until he had three months of sobriety. Unfortunately, Dylan was unable to do it, and has spent the rest of his life in and out of prison.

As far as Roxy knows today, he is still in prison. Roxy thankfully continued with therapy, in the span of five years that all this occurred. Roxy continued going to meetings, and decided to go back to graduate school, as Roxy needed to survive, and raise her children, which was out of her norm, as she never wanted to work, she always just wanted to be a mother, and have more kids. Roxy was getting stronger and stopped going to therapy when she was in graduate school. When she ran into me a few years later, she told me that she started therapy again, as she was told in graduate school that all good therapists need to go back to therapy every now and then. Roxy carried a guilt that when she married, she married for life, which was her dream, and the divorce was not only the best thing that happened, but it was the death of her dream. She then realized that a woman could survive without a man, but she dated others afterward, in the hopes that she could find a father for her children, although her children said she did a wonderful job as a mother and father. And you never know, there may still be hope.

Roxy is now a licensed therapist and a drug and alcohol counselor. This story is not even half of what Roxy has been through. She is a thriving, incredibly strong woman, with two wonderful children, and beautiful grandchildren. She is currently living on the beach, with her best friend, her dog, Ebbie, living her best life. Roxy is so grateful and thankful for every day. She adores her family and is blessed and happy. Throughout the years, when I also counseled her besides her past therapy, I focused on helping her to realize her worth and value. She took my counsel and advice and worked toward making goals, and striving to be the person she was meant to be. Roxy knows that she can achieve anything she puts her mind to. Until this day Roxy and I have never lost touch. She is doing great in her career. She is a new woman, a champion, and now lives in the winner's circle. We continue to communicate several times a year. She is doing amazingly well, her strength, love, and fortitude for her family is her driving force.

Growing pains are not easy, but Roxy's story really drives home as to the pain people experience, and how wonderful it is when we come out the other side. In Roxy's case, she sought out help from the beginning. She wanted nothing more than to be happy, be married, and have children. All that fell apart, but the most amazing thing is how Roxy is now giving back to society and helping those that are in need of help as she was. She is an amazing woman, and her story will help others to be strong, and to never give up. Thank you, Roxy, for sharing such personal and difficult times. Your story will forever help many who are hurting.

In my meditation, words kept coming to me for my reader: align yourself with the magical mystery of the glory and that is coming into your life. I thought to myself I am ready, and I believe so are you, to experience the wonderful wonders of your potential and glorious new beginnings. As I was in thought, I thought of the healing that I went through, I recalled the times when I was rejected and verbally abused. I recalled that drive in the car in New York City, how he spewed curses at me. It causes a rejection complex. When a person spews out words of hurt and pain, it is devastating to the hearer. Abuse of any kind is unacceptable, but verbal abuse cuts deep as the hearer, the recipient, endures the words from another human being that they once trusted and were close with, and that also hurts deeply, and it's pretty traumatic.

Two types of abuse people encounter include physical (hitting, punching, and much worse actions) and verbal (name-calling, shouting, and yelling). Staying in an emotionally or verbally abusive relationship can have long-lasting effects on your physical and mental health, leading to chronic pain, depression, or anxiety. Sometimes, you can go back and defend yourself, depending on the type of personality you have. Everyone is different on how they handle these encounters in their lives. Many divorces and breakups happen because of this type of abuse where they cannot longer live under the same roof. Where there is regular abuse going on, there is no restraint, there is no filter, and it continually escalates. It is imperative that you do talk to someone and do not let anyone break you down to the point of being hurt so deeply. This is one of the scarring methods to which a person begins to break down and have emotional damage such as issues of rejection and fears, which is what I am discussing and breaking down in this chapter.

AFFECTS YOU EXPERIENCE WITH REJECTION

- Feelings of being left out
- Feelings of being not wanted, especially in breakups
- Feelings of being forgotten
- Feelings of not being included
- Feelings of being skipped over

Rejection – Feeling rejected is the opposite of being accepted, the dismissing or refusing of a person, proposal, idea, etc. Rejection can be defined as the act of pushing someone or something away. One may experience rejection from one's family of origin, a friend, or a romantic partner, and the resulting emotions can often be painful. Rejection can be experienced on a large scale or in small ways in everyday life. Rejections happen to all of us every day, some bad, some not as bad. It is an effect of an internal wound that needs to be brought to the light. If not healed, in matters of affecting you deeply and interfering with your daily life, we need to find out why you are constantly feeling rejected. In some instances, and I love you, it could be the wounds are so deep internally that much of the hurt can be felt with even the littlest rejection. This hurt is real, and it is being acknowledged here in this chapter.

Questions to ask yourself:

- How often do I feel rejection?
- What keeps you up at night?
- What is the trigger, now that am aware of my emotion?
- How long does it upset me – a full day, half a day, thirty minutes?
- Is there anger associated when it triggers off?
- What do I do to continue after an episode: sleep, cry, watch tv?

Example "answers" to a few questions above:

- Two times a day
- Anytime the mention of my family comes up
- Lasts about one hour
- Yes, I get angry
- I cry then move on

Above is an example of the measure of the damage, with this, it is good to get an idea of evaluating the degree of the emotional damage this person is suffering. Rejection is based on triggers that occur when the feeling of being unaccepted and feeling left out occurs. If a person is healthy and does not have these issues, and gets rejected by a normal circumstance such a work-related rejection, then the person takes it in stride. However, deep wounds take time to heal. Verbal abuse is one of the main key factors of rejection; its sister is abandonment, so if a child was abandoned at a small age or left unattended for long periods of time, the feeling of abandonment and rejection can pop up easily and steadily. When you deal with rejection from a partner, you can go thru stages of grief, like waves.

Find a good support system for yourself and importantly, do not keep taking the blame. Set up yourself with self-care daily, and if need be and you are having a lot of difficulties, find a therapist who can help you. The feeling of being alone, and dealing with a broken relationship or divorce, can be devastating and you can question yourself constantly. You are asking yourself, "I cannot believe I have to go through this alone again. I cannot believe I have to carry this heavy load," and that causes deep grief, rejection issues, and abandonment. Like myself, I was concerned with my breakup about my raising my children, how alone and lost I had felt. I had all sorts of emotions alone, afraid of how I was going to financially survive. One thing I did, which is therapeutic, is I would have coffee with my friend or friends who I trusted – that helped me cope better. There were times when I suffered insomnia as fear gripped my heart. If you are experiencing any of this, the I pray the words of this book would be like a healing balm upon your heart.

QUESTIONS YOU MAY BE DEALING WITH AFTER BREAKUP

- How do I love myself and others again?
- How do I gain my self-worth back?
- How can I be secure again?
- How can I heal from rejection, abandonment, and verbal abuse?
- How do I find my voice again?
- How do I find my identity back?
- How do I gain my self-respect back?

I will be addressing each and every one of these questions on how to find your self-worth and identity back, feel secure, and get healing from rejection. You will be whole and find your voice again and gain your self-respect and self-esteem back. In these last few chapters, I am breaking down the emotional damage root causes so we can describe them and get to know what emotions you are dealing with. In this chapter, my focus is on knowing about rejection and its meaning, and I will call out another big elephant in the room called *fear*.

I love to break down the four letters in the alphabet of FEAR:

F: false

E: evidence

A: appearing

R: real

It is imperative that we open our hearts to the new path of living a healthy and successful life by beginning to frame your outcome where you will be learning to take time for yourself, taking walks, car rides, going to the beach, traveling, socializing, self-gratification, self-love practices, silence, meditation, learning to have non-judgmental thoughts, enjoying the outdoors, prayer, journaling daily, and taking steps to clearing a path to a more fulfilling and beautiful life. This is the path that we will be discussing after we break down the emotions that have held you back. Fear freezes people in the space of time from fulfilling their purposes and dreams. Rejection, as we have broken down this emotion, causes fears. It's time to close the door on fear.

EMOTIONS THAT OPERATE UNDER FEAR

- Anxiety
- Hopelessness
- Uneasiness
- Stress
- Phobias
- Fear of failure
- Doubt
- Fear of the future
- Nightmares
- Worry
- Inferiority
- Rejection
- Fear of death
- Panic
- Timidity
- Nervousness
- Loss of courage
- Fear of heights
- Fear of confined areas

CONSTRUCTIVE WAYS TO COMBAT FEARS

- Set an agenda to speak the opposite of the fear
- Journal when you sense the fear and be specific
- No more petition prayers: get firm and speak directly out loud to the fear
- Find a friend you can trust of professional help to talk about it with
- Get rid of negative words from the past and turn those negatives to positives

Example of turning negatives to positives using this positive affirmation exercise:

I'm not intelligent enough.

Response: I am super gifted and intelligent.

I am always financially struggling.

Response: I am financially successful, and I have more than enough.

I will never get a job.

Response: I just got the greatest job and I start tomorrow.

I will never get married.

Response: Me and my boyfriend are talking about getting married. I am so excited.

I will never get on top of my workload.

Response: I'm always ahead of the game at work and have so much time for other tasks.

I will never get promoted.

Response: I'm so excited. I sense a promotion on the way for me.

My life will always be like this.

Response: I love my life. It's so exciting every single day.

This is the way I am.

Response: I am awesome, talented, happy, and love new surprises every day.

YOU MUST CONNECT TO YOUR SOURCE OF FEAR (SMALL ASSIGNMENT)

QUESTIONS TO ASK YOURSELF ABOUT *FEAR*:

- Do you have fears? Name a few, if any.
- Have you conquered your fear or fears?
- What kind of fear is it?
- Does it debilitate you?
- How long does it last?

Have you found remedies to quiet the fear? This is a good exercise to write down and to help combat your fear. This may have to be done few times to see success, Remember, I told you words have meaning, power, and consequences.

- Name your fear
- Face your fear
- Speak to your fear, tell it what you want to say
- Tell it to go
- Mean what you say

The Power of Positive Thinking and speaking have molded generations past. It is a great tool in healing those negative words that we are accustomed to using. It is so important that we frame our worlds by the words we speak daily. The Bible says that death and life is in the power of your tongue and they that love it shall eat the fruit thereof. It is high time to denounce those words and take the realm of the new wave that is coming your way to ride it. Tell that negative thinking to each and every one go, you are not renting space in my head any longer. Simple task, simple as cherry pie. Go, get out of here, and the more you do it, the more you will come to believe. Believe and you will receive, a statement that has been around for centuries. It's been around for a reason; it's been around because it works. My desire in writing this book is that you experience joy and peace, and not fear and grief.

One time, I was in church, alone, and my children were with my mother; this was years ago when they were little. I was so bound by fear I was experiencing a hard breakup, and I needed counseling from the church, where I felt comfortable and was a regular attendee. I was crying after the sermon, not loud, just quiet no one noticed, and the pastor says from the pulpit, I remember so vividly, the pastor calls out. Now I did not know the pastor or the people well as I had only been attending there for three months. The pastor calls out, and speaks these words, "There is a woman here tonight, she has children and just went through a hard breakup, and fear is debilitating her from functioning normally. If that's you, step forward so we can pray for you." Well, I was crying already, and no one really knew me, so what did I have to lose, I asked myself. I was thinking, I know that's me, should I go up, maybe, I can always call and make an appointment with one of the pastors, and then, am thinking but what if I miss my healing. I knew being a church girl that God speaks through people and I just got up there, and I had them pray for me. It was the most beautiful experience that I had ever encountered in my life. I sensed almost like an egg being cracked over my head, like a soft yoke, being poured. I sensed an incredible peace that I never ever knew existed.

I felt elated and like I was on a cloud. I knew this was God, I knew, He knew me. The pastor and prayer team were already gone. I was just basking in the glorious glory of something so much bigger than me This was my first encounter with Source, the Living God. There is something greater than us; I knew I had a supernatural encounter. Weeks went by and I felt so much lighter, like a heavy load was taken off my shoulders. There are many avenues; the Universe, God, Source, your inner-being, will help you in your healing process. It's simple – you just have to be open to that.

Even if you are not open to the spiritual realm of the supernatural, you will encounter many blessings and healings of damaged emotions from a broken heart to grief of a loved one, to divorce or even any tragedy. Simple steps of just realizing what insecurities are, rejection, fears, unforgiveness, and more emotions that occur to us, you still can be healed, simply by your mindset, or thought pattern changing, such as positive affirmations, as I described above. Also, taking walks as we discussed, getting outdoors, and enjoying nature is healing. Take a nice long drive and have that quiet time to yourself and think about things. All these are avenues that are available. A great avenue is great book written in the subject you are experiencing difficulties in. Reading a book can transform a life. It does it to me, every time I find a good book.

The road to happiness is there for you. The question is, "Are you willing to grow, and mold into the new creation that you were purposed to be from the beginning of time?"

THE ESSENCE OF BEING GRATEFUL

One of the greatest gifts that I have experienced in my life is the gift of gratefulness. Being grateful and thankful daily opens the Universe to give you more blessings. In my positive daily confessions, I mention the things that I am grateful for. I do this daily. If busy, it's shorter, but I maintain a healthy mindset. To be able to survive, for me, this is like breathing. I am so grateful to be a mother of three beautiful sons, and their beautiful wives, and so thankful for my grandchildren. I am so thankful and grateful to be alive. In the last chapter, I will tell you more of why am so grateful to be alive, so read on.

There is a secret to being thankful and grateful. It truly opens the avenue into the universe to grant you the best there is in life. I am grateful for everything connected to me, like my car, the place where I live, the roof over my head, my health, my children's health, my job as a major airline employee, my life as an evangelist, my new career as a life coach, thankful for my Latin dance love, my dog Lolita, and so much more. These words are my appreciation and gratitude for life words. You become very grateful when you have come from welfare, and cheese and crackers.

In essence, you can receive your healing and renounce audibly and reject fear. Take the upper hand over these emotions. Look at it as, "Should I wear this dress or this one?" Simply by making a simple decision, you can train your mindset and learn to recognize and renounce any partnership. Fear must go and stop in its tracks. Close the door to fear; it has no place in your beautiful and amazing life. Value yourself more than ever before as you learn to realign by taking steps to love yourself more. You must know you were not meant to be bound by the effects of rejection and fear, as that is not part of your purpose or calling in your life. Take it by force, with the strength of your inner-being and by the power of your thought and tongue. This is called mindset deliverance and healing of damaged emotions. Begin sending new messages to yourself, love letters to yourself, and be set free once and for all. What you speak and think comes to pass, it is the law of gravity and the Law of Attraction. It is the *now*, which is important. It is believing in the moment and being happy and grateful for the gifts you already have. Make the transfer of power with the words that you speak. The mind is a powerful thing, and it listens to you.

> *"For God has not given us a spirit of fear, but of power and love and of a sound mind."*

> — 2 TIMOTHY 1:7, NKJV

A FLOWER

A flower blooms
And grows ablaze
Its beauty is extravagant,
As the sun has rays
It's delicate, it's soft,
It's feminine, it's lush
Sweet like a woman's touch
Her beauty is amazing,
The wonder of her love
A flower is beautiful,
Like you, my dove!

— MYRNA IVETTE
CLAUDIO

6

THE ROOTS OF ABANDONMENT
AND FORGIVENESS

Many people are suffering with these emotions of abandonment and rejection. These hurts affect human beings, because they hide their pain inside themselves. They come out of a person by way of anger, sickness, disease, and even abuse. This is one of the worst emotions a human suffers. Forgiveness is key to our freedom. Now, keep in mind, you really do not have to go to a person to apologize, or ask forgiveness, in order to be set free of the bitterness you hold. All that is required is quiet time and self-reflection, and words such as, "I am making a decision today to forgive and let go. I will no longer be affected or bothered by this. Today, I decide to forgive and forget, and I will release blessings unto them. I will no longer carry this burden." That is, it my friends, a quiet time of reflection, but of course, you can go to them and apologize, but the key here is not as much for them, as it is to set you, yourself free, so you can move on to higher heights, and deeper depths, and into your horizon. In these pages, we break down even more ways to be free and the root causes. So get ready – this is a beautiful thing.

Abandonment is one of the most painful of all

emotions. It is an act of leaving a person or thing for a period, or permanently. Many people struggle with abandonment. It doesn't necessarily mean that it's the end, abandonment can occur even in my story, when I spoke about my spouse, that he left me on his birthday, at a park in his car for over six hours. Why and for what reason, I will never know, but it was horrific, as I didn't have transportation and had no choice, but to be left there. I did have the keys to his car, so I did leave and go looking for him, as I said earlier in the book.

The point I am making here, is that I was abandoned, and even for a short time, that is how I felt. I had emotions of anger, fear, rejection, disgust, and abandonment. It was terrible feeling like you are not important enough for the other person to care enough to even say, "Go home ,honey. It's my birthday and I'm going for a walk for a while," or even say, "I will drive you home. I am going out with my friend Mike," and so forth. Not at all, he just walked off into the grassy field and kept walking and never came back, and as I said, I thought he was hurt, or even died. I called family, "They said he'll be back soon. I am sure he's just walking." To me, that was unforgivable. Which is what I will be focusing on in this chapter. How no matter what a person does, forgiving is key in order for us to move forward in our lives.

When a person has encountered abandonment, it creates feelings of disconnection, rejection, and trauma. It causes a fear of not only losing connection with the people you love, but being forced, especially in a breakup, to fend for yourself. Sometimes, it happens so quickly, and out of the blue, that you were not prepared for what just happened. It causes a fear that can impair a person's ability to trust again. It causes the person to feel unworthy and not be able to open up as easily and be intimate. It goes as far as people having had to go through deep depression that then, they became codependent on others. In future relationships, they even tend to be super cautious and have jealous tendencies and being overly eager to please others to aim to get acceptance in order to feel loved and accepted. At times, they try to get reassurance that even as far as friends, making sure that they really like them, needing frequent reassurance.

One of the emotional traumas caused early on in childhood years is when a parent works, and is absent for days and days, and the child is raised by others. There are other childhood traumas when the parents are physically present but emotionally absent. This happened to me; my mom was absent, as she worked when I was a child, and I was raised by my grandmother. Of course, there are many amazing parents, that work and come home and make time for their children, and do great activities to make up the time, but unfortunately, there are parents so wrapped up in work and busy lives that the children suffer the loss of their parents. It is so unfortunate to endure such a feeling. Many have never experienced it, but many reading this book have or have not, and/ or you have been through a breakup or even a bad divorce and have felt abandoned and so lost. It causes deep insecurities and loneliness that you sit and wonder what you did wrong, or what you did to deserve this, or why you find yourself alone in a place like this.

Abandonment issues can happen at any time, and for some people it begins in childhood, but for others it could have happened later in life by an abusive relationship. You may experience triggers of abandonment by losing a job, losing a loved one, or the loss of a romantic relationship. Another relationship trauma caused to a person in a relationship is being cheated on; it may take a long time to heal. It causes deep pain and anxiety, depression, and difficulty trusting others for a long time after this occurs. It causes the person to fear intimacy and being intimate again.

PATHS TO HEALING OF ABANDONMENT

- Examining the onset of the trauma
- Accepting it for what it is
- Meditation (fifteen to thirty minutes) daily
- Journaling your emotions of pain and abandonment
- Seeking help and support (nonprofessional and/or professional)
- Staying in control of your feelings
- Letting go of bad feelings
- Beginning new healthy habits
- Being good and patient with yourself

One of the main ingredients needed for healing in any of these subjects that have been mentioned in these pages, is the act of *forgiveness*. Forgiveness is truly practicing self-love. Forgiveness is a choice and a determined decision we make, and it is not so much about the person or persons who caused you hurt, but it is about you and you, alone. When I forgive, which I do at least a few times a week, or at least once a week, I do it, not because of anyone else but for me. I want to keep my heart in the purest form possible. You may have seen the movie, *The Passion*, or any other Jesus movie, where he says from the cross, "Forgive them for they not know what they do." He was right. A person who is healed, and is looking to live a healthy life with their spirit, soul, mind, and body does not hurt others on purpose or fun, or for the hell of it. A person, who knows the truth about love and walking in love or at least is trying to, does not go around hurting others on purpose. It doesn't matter if the person deserves forgiveness or not – it would be nice, to have that nice rapport – but I do it for me and my freedom of peace. There is always or in the future there will be, at times, someone you may need to forgive, or have not forgiven.

What is forgiveness? "Psychologists generally define forgiveness as a conscious, deliberate decision to release feelings of resentment or vengeance toward a person or group who has harmed you, regardless of whether they deserve your forgiveness." Once you make the decision to forgive someone or more than one person, it clears a path for you not to have it any longer in your consciousness. Once you forgive, it is done, again, remember Jesus' words; after he died on the cross that day on Calvary, his last words were, "It is finished." Yes, it is finished. You move on. One important key fact here, is you are not a mat to be stepped on by anyone. Once you forgive, you must make some mindful decisions as to what your next steps are going to be. Such as, do I continue to be around this person as if nothing ever happened? The answer could go either way. With some people, you should know internally never to be around them again and that decision is your intuition.

You must always listen to the inner voice, your intuition; it will guide you. If it says to never speak and never see them again, then that is that. Another option is, see them because I have no choice; they are always around, or I work with them, and I will just be cordial when I see them, so as not to cause further riffs in the sand, and with this choice you just see them and say, hi and bye, and never ever get personal with them. A hi and bye is all that your intuition has chosen and that is called wisdom. Especially if you know that person will never change, in this case with this choice, never tell them your business, your dreams, your comings and goings, just hello and goodbye. It's just being cordial, could be at work, or a family member who is around, and it's just the polite thing to do.

The third choice is, for someone such as a romantic partner, husband, a mother or father, or sibling, you forgive. Then you move on, and you continue your relationship, but this type of person, you speak to but you need to be alert and aware, some stripes never go away. With this type of person, even if it's a close person, create some boundaries in your inner being, that only you know about, and make sure you don't get close to them in those instances, where hurt, harm, and danger can easily occur as you may live with them. You can with this third choice, of a person that is closer in proximity, be alert and aware and as I said, be mindful to keep your heart guarded anyway, for out of it flows the issues of life, and even this close of a person, you must internally refrain from their not needing to know every single detail of your inner being. Guard your heart at all times. Those are three types of people you have forgiven, but it's your decision and your intuition for which choice you will go with. I suggest you refer to this paragraph as it is filled with gold nuggets of peace of mind and enjoying a peaceful transition of aftercare, after you have forgiven, in your reactions to each individual who you are forgiving in the aftermath of the forgiveness action.

There are cause and effects when we choose not to forgive. The negative consequences of not forgiving can lead to emotional pain, anger, hatred, hurt, bitterness, nastiness, resentment, a cold heart, and can also create sickness in our bodies. What can also happen is, when in a relationship, it can hurt the relationship as you carry all that baggage around with you. Unforgiveness does not allow us to flow in the freedom that we were as humans were meant to experience. Keep in mind that not forgiving a person, does not make you a bad person, as you need to know there are avenues available that can bring much healing such as meditation, and even quiet walks reflecting on the situation at hand. Although using forgiveness as a tool is cleansing to your soul, you don't even need to plan this long ritual. Just forgive, my simply saying, "I choose to forgive my ex-boyfriend for being so nasty and hurtful with those words. I choose to forgive him, and I release him now to go on about his life, and I chose to be free of this hurt. I will no longer carry this burden around, I am free of this pain, and he is forgiven." That's how simply it can be done.

Forgiveness is not a major ritual. It is a simple confession of faith. It is believing that I will no longer deal with these thoughts, this anger, anymore, I am done, I now forgive my aunt for not calling me like she promised me, so I choose to forgive her, and release this and her and I am setting myself free of any anger. Like I said, this is not necessarily about the other person. That's not to say that someone is not going to get you mad for a little one day. The lesson here is in the handling of these things that spoil the vine, that if we take a little time in our prayer, or meditation, or walks, and ask yourself, "Who am I upset with? What is making me angry? Why does that person bother me every time I see them, or they show up or even talk? Why do they affect me so much?" This is the time to examine your heart, ask yourself who, and why, and how come, so you can come up with anyone who has a hold or a grip in your heart. I, being human, of course, deal with things that come up all the time, but I do have this as my weekly thing to do prior to meditation, maybe not daily but at least once a week. I want to have a clean heart. How can we expect to be loved, if we can't forgive? How can we give love? Imagine, as we clear the funnel by forgiveness, how much more loving and open the funnel will be, and how much love we will have to give and receive.

It takes a special individual, and that is you, to have the

wisdom it takes, to walk in the river of love, the river of blessings, to walk in joy, and gratitude. How can you be grateful, and do these positive affirmations, and yet you can't forgive your neighbor? One of the scriptures says, "Love your neighbor, as yourself." I take that literally. Just last week, it hit me – and I am not a Bible scholar – love your neighbor as yourself. So, if I don't love my neighbor (meaning mankind); then how can I say I love myself. It does not add up. If you love yourself, then you must love your neighbor. As the Word of God states, "Love your neighbor as you love yourself." When we do we, are fulfilling one of the greatest Commandments.

PATHS TO FORGIVING YOUR NEIGHBOR (AND HUMANKIND IN GENERAL)

- Examine where the hurt is coming from and acknowledge it
- Journal and figure out how you've been hurt
- Keep in mind the past is gone, all you can do is work on yourself
- Know you cannot change the person who hurt you
- Meditate, ponder, take walks, and consider what would be your next strategy
- Figure out if you will decide to forgive this person or persons
- Forgive and make it a choice to release it
- Accept the love and healing that comes from forgiveness
- Decide which of the three choices given of continued connection with the person who hurt you will apply

AFFIRMATIVE DECISION TO FINALLY FORGIVE

The decision to forgive is easy; it is the reaction to the aftermath, and the decision you will make after you forgive, that is crucial. Like I said, you do not ever want to give anyone the opportunity to hurt you again. Make it clear in your mind and heart that you have value and are valuable. You are worthy of being happy. You are an incredible human being created to enjoy a beautiful life on this earth. You can forgive, but never forget, what people have done to hurt you, and you must make sure that you do not allow that door, that avenue to ever open again. But that is your choice and only your choice, as this is your life. It is imperative that you guard and protect your heart diligently at all times.

When we have gone through hurtful situations, verbal abuse, or breakups, it is important to learn lessons from those events that took place in our lives. There are traits that people carry, and red flags that we must look out for in our lives in order to learn to grow from those past relationships. Otherwise, guess what, they will happen again. It is strictly up to you, to spend time in reflection on the things, and those that have hurt us so deeply. Reflection is key, meditation, and self-awareness is key to journaling what occurred, what happened, why did it happen, did I cause it, what did I contribute to it, was I in the wrong place at the wrong time? These are things to contemplate for your life, to have more positive relationships in the future. Believe me, people will show you red flags, and with those red flags, you will be observant enough, experienced enough, to know, you are not going there, you are not doing that, and you are not dealing with this. Life is there for you to learn and to grow. Maybe you will be pickier in choosing who, what, where, and how, but that is great, you've been down that road before, and you are not going there again.

Once you make your decision to forgive, move on. If it comes up by a friend or a relative, and they inquire, "Hey, you still mad at so and so?" say, "No, I forgave them and I've moved on, so let's move on, as I prefer to leave the past in the past." Why bring it up over and over again? The reason I spent time in this subject, is because it is the one grip that holds your heart from being set free. Once you carry these burdens and unforgiveness, we continue to carry it into other areas of our lives. As I mentioned earlier, triggers will come up, of the person's name, or events that may remind you of the event that occurred like flashbacks of the past hurt, and it stays in there embedded in your heart. Let's get free of this, so you can move forward in creating a new life for yourself and growing in love and finding ways to be always continually truly happy and joyous. Life is short. Why not enjoy the gift of it in freedom, releasing these bondages that have held us back by not forgiving? So today, take these steps, forgive, let go, and be free once and for all. You were created for such a time as this to be set free, with no encumbrances, no hindrances, no attachments that were holding your heart bondage. Let's get free.

"And be kind to one another, tenderhearted, forgiving one another, even as God in Christ forgave you."

— EPHESIANS 4:32, NKJV

I AM

I am the Rain, I am the Sky
I am the River, so why not fly
I am the purpose for which you live,
I'm in the trees, to give you bliss
I am your Strength, I am your Love,
I am the Power from Above
I am your Peace, In which you Live,
I am that Wisdom, that I Give
I am Your Inner Being,
I am that Intuition
That Voice, that Love,
That Greater Vision.

— MYRNA IVETTE
CLAUDIO

7

DETERMINED TO BE IN THE WINNER'S CIRCLE

Being determined is a focal attitude to living your new and successful life. To be determined as a human being is to know your mark, and set your target. You must have a vision. Most of the champions and folks in the winner's circle are determined people. They know what they want, but most of all they know what they don't want. In order to know what you want, you must first know what you don't want. You cannot be living your lives, taking aim at nothing, and letting your days go undetermined. In order to be a champion and be in the winner's circle, you need to have short-term goals, and long-term goals. You must be good at time management, and goal-setting. One of the key components to being determined to win, is to be focused, and aligned with yourself, your inner-being number one, and with your aspired vision. Vision is so key to setting the target, or the mark, to where you are headed. The Word of God, in the Bible it states, "My people perish for lack of vision." People go to and from and without vision and inclusive purpose, there is no mark to attain. In these pages, we will focus on getting determined to win and be in the winner's circle. Be determined to gain a new path of recovery and learn to be determined and focused to grow and seek a new purpose in life. It is imperative to have a want, to have fire shut up in your bones. You can achieve this success, everyone can, and yes, you can.

Preparing mentally to leave a relationship, and finally making the choice to leave, is a freeing feeling. You feel freedom, and fear, and nervous at the same time of the unknown future. Like for me, one of my biggest concerns was where do I live, will I be able to afford a place to live on my own? How do I do this on my own? How do I start over? I finally did it, I found an apartment and left him, and I did not look back. My mom who lived with me for several years prior to this, was now in a more advanced stages of dementia, so she went back to a professional dementia home in Puerto Rico. That was a rough, a few years, of living with my mom with dementia, and going through years of being separated from Jeremy. After his last heart surgery, we became more and more apart. I never attempted to go see him after work or try to have dinners with him any longer.

After the hospital suicide incident, I stopped trying, I was emotionally done with the relationship. He never came home until late hours. He would still do our food shopping, and at this point, it was just one child in the home living with me and all grown up now, and we never saw Jeremy during the day. I went to a lawyer and served him with divorce papers. It was over and I was numb. The love I had for him slowly faded away. The less I saw him, the less I felt. Until, finally, I moved out to my new place. It took time for me to adjust, there were nights where I experienced such anxiety that I could not sleep.

However, I just kept pressing on and on. As I was going forward in my new life, my job continued giving us employees raises, and thankfully things were going in an upward movement, they kept increasing, and things seemed as if I was going to be fine. I felt at times lonely and alone. I'm so thankful that my children are close to me, and I have them to love; I am so grateful. Jeremy still would not come home during the day but, we were separated at this point. Prior to me leaving, he continued to sleep in our bedroom, as I slept in the large living room we had, and my mom and I shared those living quarters.

I needed to see him one day and told him, I would pass by his job after work. He worked at an office building in the back of the main electrical plant. I pulled up and I see his car and another car parked next to his car. I called, as I couldn't just walk in, to let him know I was outside, and a girl runs out frustrated and mad. She looked as if I interrupted something. She was there alone with him. He came out white as a ghost, and I said not one word. We'd been separated for almost a year, so I just up and left – I drove away.

I had no feelings, no anger, no emotion. For the first time, I waited up for him, after midnight, he walked into the room, and he asked me, what are you doing in here, you never come in here, I said who was she, I'm not stupid, and he turned ignored me and went to take a shower. Enough said, there were no words. That was the first time, when I knew without a shadow of a doubt that I needed to leave and not turn back. I went to bed planning my way out, I was sad, happy, confused, shocked, and numb. I may have been numb, but I was certainly not dumb. For the first time in my life, I had a door wide open to leave once and for all. It was like the first day of the rest of my life.

Have I forgiven Jeremy? Yes, I have. I did it a while ago.

I do not want to carry any more chains, not from him, not from anyone. I didn't know where to go, so my first pit stop, was a divorce attorney. Next stop was church, and next was planning my way to my new life. I didn't know how, where, and what my next steps were, but sometimes you need to trust your intuition; it does not lie. Your intuition, your inner voice, your inner being, is set up inside of us like a GPS, showing us where to go and not to go. Sometimes, we take the wrong turns, because we don't even know we have a GPS built inside of us. How do you get to learn how to use it? I learned by meditation, and being keenly aware of my instincts, which will always guide us. I was ready to go into the unknown, but I knew I had to go.

That prompted me to stop being in that living room and make the steps necessary to bring my mom to her sister's in Puerto Rico. I made the appointment with a lawyer, and thank God, took a girlfriend of mine with me. My lawyer lady was incredibly smart, and had those papers drawn right away. He was served, and came home and said these words, "Thank God. This is like a weight being lifted off my shoulders." Unreal, twenty-two years of marriage, and that is what he said.

I'm now moved into my apartment and gathering myself, as I begin enjoying going to work, and living my life. I am asking myself questions such as how I start my life again after this breakup and divorce, how do I get my security back, how I get rid of these lonely feelings, how do I get my identity and self-worth back. I had this all going through my mind. At this time, I realized that I needed healing, I needed a clear path to restore my life back. I was having trouble resting at night as I had been experiencing fears of being alone for the rest of my life, and fear of what the future holds for me now. I was experiencing such responsibilities by myself and wondering how things were going to work out. I was concerned I would go into a depression, and I cannot afford to lose my job now. I recall Jeremy saying, "You're uglier than Juanita," which brought up feelings, of how would I ever meet someone if am not pretty enough. These were evil thoughts attacking my mind. I knew I had to snap out of it and get myself to a better place.

DETERMINED TO WIN THIS FIGHT

I began reading my Bible, went for walks, and started to learn I was worth who I am. It took a few years for me to come to a place of emotional healing. I read books on saying positive things about myself. I found books on wellness, and self-help books, and I started little by little to sense a love for myself that I had lost with relationships that broke me. I was on my path to recovery. I knew I had a long way to go, but I was so determined to be whole and not allow my sadness to bring me to depression. I was already determined and believing that I could have purpose in my life. I continued to grow spiritually and continued reading books to lift my soul.

My children were all grown, and two are now married, and the youngest in a beautiful relationship. For a mother, there is nothing more rewarding than seeing your children be happy and succeeding in life. It was a good feeling to know that my relationship breakups, instead of hurting them, it made them so strong, that they don't want to see that in their relationships. Now I'm well on my path to recovery and wellness. My friends would say to me, "It's been a year since your divorce – you should date." I just ignored that thought, I focused more on my job, and decorating my apartment and making it nice. I felt I've come a little further, to have a strange man break this little bubble of mine, to me seemed ludicrous. Well, six months went by, and I did go on an online site and dated casually a few people, nothing serious, and I decided to stop and just focus on me.

I was determined to get stronger and stronger. I had

now been working for a major airline, and I traveled. I went with girlfriends to Paris, Jerusalem, Nice, France, and of course, visited my island of Puerto Rico quite often to see my mama, Betty. My dad had passed already now more than five years. She missed him so much, so did I, and all my children did also. My spirits were lifted, and mind was still determined to grow into a better person. It is a beautiful road, but you don't get there, unless either you are called in a special way, or you are just determined to get there. Some people stay where they are by choice. I chose the road to greatness.

Determination: firmness of purpose or resoluteness. Specifically, being determined means have a firm decision or goal and not wavering in your pursuit of achieving it.

A determination can be a decision or just the focus that you must get something done. Some people, or this could have been me, where I could just stay status quo, and live my life dealing with the triggers of insecurities, rejection, fear, abandonment, unforgiveness, all of which were broken down in the previous pages of this book. Why is determination so important in our wellness and recovery? It is because it enables us to go on to pursue, to persist in the midst of hardships and difficulties. It helps us to go forward, and march ahead with faith, so we can conquer and achieve our goals. Having determination gives us stamina, courage, and helps us to overcome daily situations that arise. It helps us persevere in difficult obstacles that may try to hinder us. Determination is key to your growth, as it is important to never give up and never give in. I thought to myself, "I've been through enough with these breakups and the emotional rollercoaster of a life, that I am going to be determined to pursue my happiness. If I don't do this for myself, no one else will."

FIFTEEN KEY STEPS TO DEVELOP
DETERMINATION

- Set personal and/ or career goals.
- Think positive thoughts of yourself
- Journal and mark down your strengths
- Check your goal progress regularly
- Use online tools, books, spiritual guidance for growth
- Persevere and never quit
- Be flexible with yourself
- Give your self-rewards or credit for the things you accomplished
- Have self-gratification me time
- Be kind and gentle with yourself
- Be in the moment and present
- Have a support system of friends and loved ones
- Speak positively into your destiny with positive affirmations
- Step outside of your comfort zone without fear

It is important to know to continue on your journey to be determined to win, every day of your life, and although it can be at times be difficult remind yourself of who you are, always fix your crown when it is crooked. When you are determined to meet those goals, you win, even when it is hard or at those times that you are being tested. At the end of the day, you are there, a breathing, loving, beautiful soul, who is successful, positive, persevering, kind, in the moment, a person who walks with her head up high, not answering to everyone's beck and call, but to yours, who is now the person in charge of your life and destiny. Hold your head up high, wipe the mascara off your face, fix those broken heels, and raise your head up high to the sky.

PURPOSE FOR LIVING

Purpose is the reason for which something is done or created, or for which something exists. Your purpose and vision in life is, generally, like a destination you are achieving to get to. In preparation, goal setting is key and important for keeping yourself on a path to succeed by acquiring those goals. Vision gives us a purpose and avenue for where you are headed. It takes determination and steps to get there. What if you don't know what your vision is? Then, it is when you pray and seek for a vision, or meditate in a quiet reflection. Your vision will help you put together long and short terms goals and show you the way. Why is vision so important? It is important because it is like a target that you set up for yourself. Many souls that are without vision wander aimlessly about without purpose and vision. It is important to develop habits of wellness and healthy living. In the next few chapters, I will be breaking down in more detail habits of wellness and healthy living in creating a more positive life and striving to live your best life.

JEREMY'S AT REST

By now, Jeremy passed away, from his heart condition. I was called by his cousin, and he told me he passed, and it really crushed me. I truly loved him, although, I tried to numb that love, and I wanted to have that perfect marriage. It all went downhill with us when he shared that he would be eating dinners at his mom's house. I felt, now that I really look back, I had no chance in this marriage. I asked if I could go to the funeral services, and they said there weren't any, and that he was buried at a certain cemetery and that's it. That broke my heart, that I knew a man that I loved, he passes, and I wasn't even told until weeks later. I felt so crushed, that no matter what he did to me that I did still love him, and felt a deep loss, it took me several months to get over him.

When you are married, or have a relationship with someone, there is a spiritual closeness and connection. Two souls were once tied together spiritually. Sometimes even when the person is not close, or no longer living, the other person experiences that soul connection and deep pain like I did. I loved Jeremy much. I'm now reflecting, healing, and making strides, and continuously attempting to chart my path to wellness, becoming more determined to be whole and well. I have been daily doing my journaling, setting short- and long-term goals, persevering and pressing forward. What truly helped me in my recovery is spending quiet time with myself and truly examining my life, my ways, and without beating myself up, using those past experiences as new lessons that I have learned.

One of the key lessons about hurts and past experiences is truly learning from them. If we continue to live without reflection, how will we grow and how will we learn to be a better person? I have had much time to reflect, and of course, I work, but when I have days off, I try my best to be the person I desire to be, more positive, more giving, more kind, less judgmental, more loving, and especially wiser. Wisdom, the Bible says, is the principal thing. People can have knowledge and intellectual schooling, and have no street smarts, or have no wisdom, because wisdom is the ability to use knowledge (you learned in school) wisely.

In Proverbs 8:11 – (NKJV), one of my favorite scripture, it states, "For wisdom is better than rubies, and all the things one may desire cannot be compared with her." So beautiful – I am a huge fan of wisdom. I pray for it every single day of my life. With knowledge, I can pick up a book, I can study myself silly, but with wisdom, I can apply the knowledge in a mighty and powerful way. It's the thing, which says to the person, mover, the Universe, God, move, scoot over, I am taking over. It just gives me goosebumps. It continues here in verse twelve here, Proverbs 8:12 (NKJV): "I, wisdom, dwell with prudence, and find out knowledge and discretion." Amazing wisdom will go into the corners of everything and look for knowledge and discretion. I don't just want to be so educated with degrees and head knowledge, I want to be so educated with degrees, and have wisdom find me, and all the knowledge I put in my brain from school, and find me and look for me, so I can have the wise counsels of the Universe on how to apply that knowledge.

In this chapter, you have come far from all of those emotions that were breaking you down to now making room for a new and brighter future. I'm ready now to apply and make the path for myself to grow and to reach for the stars and the galaxies above in the Universe, for as many as there are galaxies in this amazing Universe, there is wisdom, on how to heal our broken hearts from breakups and losses, and we can grow and be determined, having a purpose and vision, to make our crooked paths straight. Fear not my lovely one, the moon and the stars and the galaxies and planets have all been aligned, as the ocean knows where to stop at its tract, at the shores of the earth, you are also being aligned with new purpose, vision, and power.

"Now to Him who is able to do exceedingly, abundantly above all that we ask or think, according to the power that works in us."

— EPHESIANS 3:20, NKJV

MY SUNSHINE

A Ray of Sunshine,
You are to Me
I give you Light,
So please be Free
I Am Bright, Am Airy,
My Light is Strong
Don't Hide away,
From Me too Long
My Light brings Healing,
Love, Peace and Joy
So please be Happy,
Am here, enjoy.
It's there for you,
So Enter In
New days begin!

— MYRNA IVETTE
CLAUDIO

8

ON THE OTHER SIDE OF
THE MOON

On the other side of the moon, which is reflective of saying the other side of the spectrum, this is a good place to see and envision, where you want to be, how you want to be, and how you will get there. It's going to take purpose, vision, determination, and a good down-to-earth attitude. This is where you will clear your calendar, you will stand your ground, you will make your changes known, and you will gain clear focus. In these pages here, you will gain clarity and understanding of the beautiful, bestowed gifts we all have – such as gratitude, thankfulness, self-worth, self-gratification, self-love, forgiveness, deliverance – and begin your pathway to healing and total freedom, and to explore the many blessings that are ahead of you. Your destiny awaits you. It will take a good attitude, faith, belief, and trust. Your destiny awaits you and now you are gaining momentum and are on the other side of the moon. You will glow, and you will flow freely and go about your life, not just focused on others, but focused on you and your purpose and vision. Remember, if you get this, you get it all: the focus is on you – you are the cake, the other people and other things, are the frosting on the cake. Never forget that because if the cake is good, all is good. You are the master of decisions in your life. Stop allowing others to continually make decisions for you, that is unless you want to and agree to the decision, but aside from that never, ever, allow others to tell you how to live your life. It is your life and only yours. Even in relationships, no one owns anyone. We are gifts bestowed to others, and a high respect must be given to that person and vice versa in relationships. You are not property; you are a gift. Learn your worth, learn who you are, stop being a yes person, be a no or yes person, but the decision must always be yours. Take your authority once and for all. This is your life.

It is now time now to move from all that held us back, all of the emotions, which have encapsulated us into the corner, and made us frozen in time. It's now time to look on the other side of the moon. The time has come for healing of damaged emotions. Time to enter into the feeling good and happy state of life, which will remove all resistance, bad moods, and situations.

The mind is a wonderful thing. It allows us to grow and the most wonderful thing about the mind – and our thoughts – is that we can self-direct, and change our thoughts at any time we want to or need to. That in itself is a powerful tool. It is a training mechanism of purposeful thoughts and thoughts bring on emotions. We have the power in us to train our thoughts and immediately say, "No, I will not give to that thought any space in my head to rent." If you can use that tool, in many instances in your life, why not use it for healing of your emotions?

In the previous chapters, we broke down and went into detail explaining and examining the emotions of insecurity, fear, abandonment, rejection, and it was broken down in a way that you can understand how and why we experience these emotions, from breakups, divorces, loss, and all kinds of hurts. Once we are hurt, the reactions to the actions that caused our hurts caused all of those emotions. In these next couple of chapters, we are turning the page, and we are opening the door of our hearts and minds to bring forth the path to realizing a new life of success, freedom, love, and unspeakable joy.

IT STARTS WITH A GOOD ATTITUDE

You have been so crushed for so long, that sometimes you feel as though the mentality is, "It is, what it is;" I say, "No, it's not. It's not what it is, it is what you create it to be." I use that term, "It is what it is," but in this case, it doesn't have to be what it is, it can be so much better. We can never reach our full potential if we say those words. As if I'll take it or leave it. We need an attitude, adjustment, an oil change, or even better, a spiritual cleansing of any negative attitude. Attitude is what will drive you to greater heights and deeper depths. With a "so what" attitude, it's as if it really doesn't matter what I do. With that type of attitude, there will never be growth in your being. It is key, for our healing process, to have the attitude of a lion, a tiger, an eagle, not a chicken attitude.

You have to want it bad enough that you taste it. Life is free for the living, and there for us to love daily and experience beautiful things, like nature, like rivers, and roaring oceans, good friends, happy times, traveling, vacationing, or even just enjoying a nice walk, or an afternoon with a friend. Life is a gift, and it is not a promise given to us. I certainly do not want to walk around as a sour lemon around my loved ones. I want to live, I want to excel, I want to be free, I desire to be happy, healthy, and wise. You can move mountains if you want to. How is your attitude, your disposition? Having a beautiful attitude is really not hard to do, all you have to do is just have it. You don't have to work at it, you just have to be in a state that you desire to have a good and pleasant attitude. Believe me, those around you will notice it, and be thankful.

In essence, a bad attitude is just like a bad mood. The important thing here is you have to want to have a good attitude, which is an example of training the mind as a tool. It is supernaturally magical.

MINDFUL STEPS TO YOUR HEALING PROCESS

- Having a good attitude
- Prayer
- Having gratitude and thankfulness
- Strong belief and faith
- Remove judgmental ways
- Staying clear of negative people and influences
- Forgive regularly
- Enjoying quiet time with nature
- Practice positive affirmations
- Mirror love
- Exercise (such as walks, healing)
- Reading positive uplifting books
- Listening to positive leadership
- Staying centered and focused
- Trust your inner voice, your intuition
- Setting short- and long-term goals
- Being organized
- Schedule good time management
- Know that hurt people, hurt people
- Draw the good from within
- Be kind and flexible with yourself
- Love humanity
- Delight in yourself
- Do not overthink things
- Release the old, make room for the new

- Get rid of clutter
- Be happy, be free
- Socialize and enjoy life
- Have a servant's heart
- Be open to learn
- Be strong and courageous
- Don't procrastinate
- Rejoice in other's blessings
- Be you, be real
- Journal daily
- Speak highly of yourself
- Guard your heart

To give a small background of myself in the way I view my spiritual life, I was raised as a Catholic school girl. I was always hungry for more than I had, spiritually. I was born in Puerto Rico, and we moved to New York, when I was just around seven years old. We kept moving back and forth; my parents were still undecided where to settle. After a long while, we did the normal Catholic communion, confirmation, and all the sacraments. As I got older, experiencing these difficult breakups, and divorces, I cried out to God and I said, "If you are real, show yourself to me." I was in my room, one day, reading a Christian book, I do not recall name of book, as I regularly read many books, in found in these pages a prayer of salvation to bring healing and deliverance to my life. I read it, and it read it out loud, and right as I finished reading it, it felt as if I swallowed air, as if something, like a light, came inside of me.

The prayer was simple, I now say it with my loved ones, or if someone is in need of a miracle or a miraculous intervention. This prayer turned my whole life around. This is my version of the prayer for a miracle turnaround, and this is what I prayed. You do not have to pray this. This is what

I prayed, this was what turned my life around 365 degrees. Now mind you, there are many avenues to healing, such as meditation, and more ways as I listed above, but I wanted to share my life experience, and how supernaturally, my life turned, as I want to be as open and transparent in this book as I can be. The prayer is below, feel free to pray it if you'd like is:

THE SALVATION PRAYER

*Prayer of Deliverance and Salvation for Those That
    need It*
Jesus, I have not been myself lately,
*Jesus, I need intervention, I am in need of your
    divine help,*
*I need a miracle, and I need a transformation in my
    life,*
*I have been doing things my way all along, I need
    you and*
*your angels of mercy and grace to intervene for my
    life.*
I know that you are real,
I acknowledge that you died on the cross on Calvary,
*And I need healing, I need change, I need salvation,
    I need*
*supernatural intervention from you, God, my
    Source.*
*I need to find my way to a better life, for better
    living,*
health, prosperity, healing, and divine intervention.
Can you step in, Lord, and help me,

> *in my life, in my job, in my circumstances, with my*
> > *family*
> *and loved ones? Can you heal us? Can you*
> > *heal me?*
> *I ask you now, my Lord, I say this prayer from my*
> > *being and my heart,*
> *Jesus come into my heart, make me whole, make*
> > *me new,*
> *make me have a clear path in my life, so that I can*
> *move forward into my destiny, with new creativity,*
> *happy, free, joyful, healthy, and at peace.*
> *Thank you, Lord, in Jesus' name, I pray. Amen.*

Prayer is a beautiful way that not just Catholics, but Christians, communicate with their God. Prayer is simply not necessarily chanting same words over and over; it is a communication with a powerful Source that listens to you. I say my prayer, whenever and however I want. I have a relationship with the Living God. I just talk like I am talking to my best friend. It is so refreshing and healing and powerful, and as you keep a journal, put in those prayers, and soon put AP – Answered Prayer, next to it. That's my initials for answered prayers. My experience with the supernatural God, is another book. He is my life, my world, my being.

Prayer is not the only way in the list above of mindful steps to your healing process; there are many ways, which will be broken down. I then, after saying that prayer above, continued on with my life. I was married and had three amazing sons, Ronald Edward, Michael Sean, and Leonard Stephen; they make my world a better place each and every day of my life. I live for my boys. Those boys were raised in the church and mama became an ordained evangelist. I did fourteen years of a home Bible study, and I was raising my sons. I kept going strong. One of the greatest gifts on earth is having tenacity that no matter what, you keep on keeping on.

One of my desires in writing this book, is to instill in my reader that tenacity, that positive life-giving spirit. Too many people give up too quickly, just when the answer is around the corner. One of the secrets to success, is living a positive and purposeful life with vision. It is having habits that work for you. A habit done on a regular basis creates success. My belief system grew from just being a Catholic believer to a born-again believer in Christ. I had given my life to God. I had served him in the Church, in my home, and created a strong spiritual foundation that could not be shaken or moved by any winds that came to shake the foundation nor by any winds that came to shake me. I changed drastically and grew to a deeper level and will be sharing the evolution of my spiritual growth. Once there, I will share my evolution. We are a spirit, we have a soul, and we live in a body.

TIME TO BUILD YOUR DESTINY

As we progress in growth, we have to focus on our destiny. Our destiny is a place we pursue. Some believe in the sovereign will of God; for others, it is man's choice. In order to fulfill our destiny, we must make the right decisions and choices. Some believe that we are destined already, and it is already a written plan for us. Whatever the case, it is important to plan to have a good and pleasant destiny. There are however people that live their lives as nomads, a people having no permanent home but moving from place to place, usually in search of food or to graze livestock. To this day, there are people without purpose, vision, or destiny such as nomads. It is lifeless, with no purpose for living, and no hope for the future. They have no goals, no intention of a purposeful life. We do not want to be described with any closeness to that word nomad. Proverbs 29:18 (KJV): "Where there is no vision, the people perish." Purpose and vision bring life and life more abundantly. Allow yourself to dream again; you were meant be on this earth, and you were born for greatness. Be ready, let the journey begin. It begins with first having gratitude, thankfulness, strong belief, and faith. When you move with a grateful heart, the Universe hears you, and aligns with your inner being, and the Law of Attraction begins to work. Having a thankful heart and a strong belief and faith are the most powerful keys to the beginning of the creation of your dreams to come true. Remember that success is a journey and not a destination. In order to create this new life, it takes discipline, it takes faith, and belief. It is time to take life by the horns, just like the Nike commercial, "Just Do It."

GRATITUDE AND THANKFULNESS

In my life, there has always been a fire, a conquest, a hunger for truth. Many people may give up on us, but we must never give up on ourselves. It is imperative that we have the unction, the drive, the get-go, the fire, to pursue the new life that you have always dreamed of having. That is why having a good attitude helps with your gratitude. Instead of complaining about where you live, or where you work, begin now to change like we spoke about, our thinking patterns, and yes, you can do that – that is, like I said, the magic of the mind. How about you walk in your apartment or house and say, wow, I love my home, this is so nice and cozy, I love being here. When you sit on the couch, say, "This couch is comfortable, and I am so thankful for it."

When you lay down to bed, be thankful for your bed, and wake up with a good attitude and a grateful heart.

Believe me, do that with your job and wherever you go, and you will notice changes. The law of reciprocity and of attraction is creating the life you speak and think about. Sometimes you just may not be in the mood. It is a funnel like a pipe that flows the desires you think about, and it flows, or it doesn't flow. You can clog the flow of miracles and manifestations of your prayers and desires with a negative mindset. Being grateful is key for more avenues of answered requests to come flowing freely into your life. Imagine just getting out of bed and trying that gratitude for a full day. Try it and see if you see breakthroughs. I did, and I'm loving every minute of it. I don't concentrate all day and do that, but if I have free time, I do it at times. A great benefit of being and living with a grateful heart and attitude is that things just seem to flow and the less complaining and clogging your pipe, the more the breakthroughs occur. Have good thoughts of people around you, and less judgment, and you will naturally see them being nicer, or even getting a promotion. It happens, it's called energy. The energy you give, is the energy you will get back.

STAYING CLEAR OF NEGATIVE PEOPLE AND INFLUENCES

Sadly enough, I have had people in my life, who say they love me, but have a negative energy and vibe. It is so important to grow, and we are like seeds that need watering. We are humans that require water, sunshine, love, and touch. It is so painful, when people you trust and love hurt you, by either their words, or their wrong judgment of you, or the lack of respect they show. It is painful when you trust people and they hurt you in such ways. Another way of being hurt by them is their ignoring the fact that you exist at all. That is more painful than anything.

The best way to heal and to grow, is unfortunately, sometimes you have to guard yourself, and stay clear of such people. Some of these individuals have no filter, and do not care about you or me. I am so glad that I have learned that I do not need them. If they do not respect or appreciate me, I move on as happily as I would if they loved me. Why? Because I am set free from the spirit and emotions of rejection. My desire is that you take this with you at the end of this book. Have a backbone. You do not need anyone. You need you. You need God, Universe, your inner being – that's true love.

Stay clear of negative people and influences. We can go on with our lonely selves, and seek their company and continue getting hurt – not me, not now, and not ever. That, you can take to the bank. I need to have me; you need to have you. You need to be happy, free from hindrances, and encumbrances, and chains that people put around us. Be free of people who mock you and belittle your dream. Forgive them and move on; as I mentioned, you forgive for you. You release them and move on. You do not have to hang around the same people who hurt you before. It's like a dog going in circles after its own tail.

You are not who they say you are, you are a queen or king. You are royalty. You have to begin to see yourself with value. You are made for such a time as this to be destined for power, majesty, and greatness. The problem we have with ourselves is we do not know who we are. We lost our way, we lost our identity, we are made in the image of God. We are the building of God, it's in the Bible. We don't decree and declare any of this because we don't know that we are meant to live a life full of purpose, vision, and destiny.

We discussed in a previous chapter that *determination* is key. But it is imperative that you realize that discipline in your faith and belief, and in having gratitude and thankfulness, gives us the key and the power to gaining the path to a new life for yourselves. Don't relent, don't give up, don't give in. Step into your destiny and learn these life lessons or things will just continue to occur. Be true to yourself, start now – it begins with a good attitude. Little by little, step by step, start with these few steps laid out in this chapter, as we continue to add on in the next few chapters, on the journey to freedom and abundant living.

> *"Therefore if any man be in Christ, he is a new creature, old things are passed away, behold, all things are become new."*
>
> — 2 CORINTHIANS 5:17 NKJ

RAIN

Shower me with Your Many Waters,
Like a River glistens,
you have always listened
A River Flows, not Knowing,
Where it Goes,
Oceans Roar the sound of Thunder,
Together they cover the Earth,
As we suffer from Hunger
Hunger goes Deep,
As we wait to be Fed
The Love that awaits,
Hoping to be Met
Storm Hits the Window Pane
Lightning and Thunder
Crashes in the Rain,
That takes away our Hunger
Showers of Rain,
Brings Freshness the Next Day,
As we Heal, Like a Miracle,
From All of the Pain.

— MYRNA IVETTE CLAUDIO

9

FINDING THE ONE TRUE LOVE

Finding your direction, and your true north, your target, is difficult for someone who has dealt with a broken heart, broken spirit, and brokenness in general. Broken relationships, divorce, or loss, causes feeling of abandonment, loss, fear, rejection, heartache. It is important to press in and pursue and want to be healed. Negativity breeds negativity, and positivity breeds positivity. Take ahold of the reins in your life and want to be happy again. It is found in finding the one true love, which I have mentioned prior is your inner-being: your Source, your God, your Universe, who adores you more than anything. They are for you and are always rooting for you. The Bible says, "If God be for you, who could be against you?" Whether you see God as God, or the Universe, or some call it Higher Power, there is only one Source. That Source is for you and loves you intensely and deeply. The key herewith now, is you finding your inner-being and falling in love, with you, you matter, you rock, and you are worth all of the sands on the beach, and the hairs on everyone's heads, all of the stars in the sky, and all of the galaxies, made for your vision. You are important, you matter, you need to come to a revival of self, and a revolution of oneness with your inner-being. May you be filled with resurrection power and new joy in your newfound life.

When you are aligned with your center, and your inner being, you feel your power of influence. The inner being knows you, loves you, and will make paths to get you to your destiny. It will not let you or go the way of resistance. We are now at a pivotal point in this book, of where you felt, I need to get my life sorted, so I can move forward, or you may feel I need to get my identity back after leaving my abusive relationship.

LIVE IN THE MOMENT AND LEARN THE POWER OF NOW

Living in the moment is key to living a successful life. *Yesterday* is gone, it is forever gone. It will not come back. The gift of yesterday is memories that we have that we can cherish forever. Another great benefit about yesterday is that you can learn lessons from it. Yesterday is the place in time in which, good or bad, it made you who you were today. Without the paths of yesterday, you could not have learned, and had those experiences, which brought you here today. With those experiences from yesterday, you can now say yes, or no, with a clear firm standing on those ways you have learned. Life is a gift, life is a blessing, life is a privilege. From yesterday, we can learn what our mistakes were, and we can learn from the past, and that makes us a better person today.

Too many people are stuck in the past. They cannot grow to become who they were intended to be. If we do the same thing and end up in the same place, making the same mistakes, that's the definition of insanity: not changing and always seeing the same results.

We need to learn and grow from our mistakes we made

even in relationships, as life gives us new chances to make things better. We have to learn from those mistakes and in learning, we have the gift of second and even third chances. Yesterday's gone, and it is something that will always be a part of us. Secondly, we have *today*, I always say, today is the present, (like a gift); and it's a beautiful thing to be in the *moment*. Take a deep breath in and out, take a few deep breaths and as you do, this is your gift, there it is, it is called the breath of life. This is the only moment that is promised to you. That breath, that inhaling, in and out, is the gift of the life-giving love. My friends, family, and loved ones, nothing is ever promised to us, except the gift of life in that moment that you breathe. We need to be so ever thankful that we can breathe and are able to experience life in its fullest. All of the other stuff about life is the frosting on the cake, but the cake, is the life, the gift of life, this moment now. Live your best life today, right now, this moment.

That is the reality of life. Life is a gift, it isn't a right, it isn't an ownership, it is a blessing, and a privilege. A sunrise in the morning is a blessing, a gift to another day. Life is so amazing and incredible that we need to come to a new place in realizing, that this is a gift that I have, and I want to live my best life *now*. It's time to go take time for yourself, and begin to live the life you have always wanted. So go to the ocean, hear it roar, hear the birds chirp, be in nature, buy those shoes, be with friends and loved ones, work hard in your job and business, take the drive, write the book, take those dancing lessons, do the movie, forgive the unforgivable, take the cruise, take the trip, hike the mountain, swim in the river of life.

We have to be so thankful and grateful with the relationships that are in our lives, to nourish them, to use kindness with people around us – your smile may be the only smile they have received in years. Hope for tomorrow is believing in faith, and knowing that God is in control. I drive on this subject with strong belief and conviction, in the hopes that you will see the importance of living in the now, and knowing that life is for the living. In this, you are living the now, the present (the gift). It is time to come into the present. You can have memories of your past, you can have dreams, goals, and faith for your tomorrows, but we must live life *now*. In essence, your gift, your present, is *now*. Take that deep breath and experience your new life. There is a beautiful Scripture passage that I love in Psalms 118:24 (NKJV): "This is the day the Lord has made; We will rejoice and be glad in it." Trust in you, trust in love, trust in the Law of Attraction, it's there for the asking. Always keep in mind the Universe can only give you the vibe and thoughts you are offering, so think wisely.

All that you want in life, you have to want it *now*, and you have to believe it, that's all. The secret sauce is I'm going to be as joyful, blessed, and happy as I can be, and as often as I can. That's the key, because like I mentioned, we are not living in the past, in the yesterdays, or in the future, the tomorrows. We live as eternal beings, *now, in the now*, forever into eternity. When you receive your answered prayer or manifestation, guess what? You will be receiving that day, and that day, will be in the *now*. All that stuff, whatever that stuff maybe, it's not about that, and it's not about the future either, it's about now, now, now. We are eternal which means we never finish. We have *now* forever. Like I mentioned, take a breath, that's the breath, now, and tomorrow, that's the breath tomorrow, and it will be in the *now*. In essence, that was then, and this is *now*, and my friends, the *power is in the now*. This is the art of feeling good: enjoy the journey, don't focus on the destination – it can be a bit of waiting and it can get you frustrated – enjoy the journey, enjoy the love, enjoy the *now*.

THE LAW OF ATTRACTION

The Law of Attraction produces physical outcomes in the real world. In this subject, I write from my experiences, I do not proclaim to be a scholar, but instead a student who is hungry for growth and success in every area of my life and being. What you ask for, you get. It is important that you have an open mind, and good attitude, and that you have a hunger to grow and learn. Without having a belief and a positive outlook on life, it will contradict all of which I am about to write here in these pages, which are filled with love from my heart.

The Law of Attraction is so incredibly amazing. It really does work. Years ago, I would hear about the Law of Attraction, but now it has become a trending subject. I read books from Abraham and Jerry Hicks, Rhonda Byrne, who wrote The Secret, and other incredible books. These books truly are something I would suggest, to live a more positive and satisfying life. Prayer is important and it is so amazing for God to hear our prayers and supplications. The Law of Attraction is different: we are not asking for something, we are believing in the present, in the now, that what we ask for, is already done for us. You must believe you have already received it. You must know it is already yours for it to manifest. This is so incredible how closely the Law of Attraction is so closely related to the Bible as it states in Mark 11:23-24 (NKJV): "For assuredly, I say to you, whoever says to this mountain, be removed and be cast into the sea, and does not doubt in his heart, but believes that those things he says will be done, he will have whatever he says. Therefore, I say to you, whatever things you ask when you pray, believe that you receive them, and you will have them."

That is so profound, that in the Bible it states in that amazing passage of Scripture, "Whatever things you ask when you pray, believe that you receive them, and you will have them." In the Law of Attraction, we ask, believe, that we have it now, and now, is the secret, that brings forth the manifestation. Many books have been written on this. I wanted a certain kind of vehicle, and I began to see myself, in my imagination, with it. Two days later, I drove away from a car lot that had my car there, and I am now the proud owner of a beautiful Range Rover. I could not afford anything close to that, but it worked out for me, with my car trade, God, and the Universe made it happen.

Miracles are waiting for you, you just need to be positive, have high vibrations, remove negativity while meditating, ask, believe, and receive. All your creative juices are awaiting in your subconscious mind, to be awakened, and to come alive. You need to come alive, to have faith, and to trust your instincts.

Basically, we have a conscious and subconscious mind. The conscious mind is the one we use for thinking and reasoning. The subconscious mind stores all our thoughts, ideas, and it has information in there from when you were a baby, a young girl, teenager, and now a grown-up. It is like a container, or a pot of gold. So, when you have a thought, your subconscious mind remembers, and immediately begins to co-create with your desired thought, to bring it to manifestation. God, the Universe, and your inner-being, meaning your subconscious mind, are all ready to begin to bring people, places, and things, to align to bring you, your answers, and dreams to reality. It is a law, and it does happen.

When you have a thought, whether a positive or a negative, the Law of Attraction only knows the now – meaning, what you are thinking now. So, it is very important that we stay free of stress and use meditation to bring calm and peace. It is so important that we begin to choose our thoughts wisely. The Law of Attraction is so very highly connected to God, in the Bible it states in Proverbs 23:7 (NKJV): "For as he thinks in his heart, so is he." It is what we think that we become, we create our world by our thoughts. Before you act, you must think. You never do anything, without a thought first being there, creating your day. When you plan your day, first you think. Before you plan your career, you think. It's all part of the desire that was already imbedded in your subconscious mind, and it was co-created by you and the Universe brought it to fruition.

It is key to continue to keep our vibrations up, and high with a positive mindset. This will allow your creativity to bring desired manifestations. A bad mood, attitude, and being judgmental toward others closes the lid on the subconscious mind to produce a positive outcome. That is why meditation plays a role alongside your inner-being, to bring you to that happy place. Miracles happen every day, you must start believing, praying, asking, and receiving. The time is now to start your new life, and a new awakening in your spirit-being. Begin to have dreams and visions, to set those goals, to daydream, to journal, to believe that you can reach your destiny.

ELIZABETH'S STORY: DIRECTOR OF NURSING, MBA, BSN, RN

I am ever so grateful to share my experience as it relates to loss and recovery of my human spirit. My loss event occurred many years ago while married with four children. I experienced a horrendous loss that encompassed loss of love, trust, security, self-worth, and self-direction. This loss allowed me to experience the well-known famous stages of grief which are denial, anger, bargaining, depression, and acceptance.

I don't want to focus this chapter on the loss event, but

on the recovery. It is having been through the experience, the storm shall I say, that I am the strong, determined, and successful woman that I am today. The event caused a cascade of events that forced me to rise-up and walk through the storm and into the sunshine.

Acceptance is key to growth and progress. You must accept the event, the loss. Once you accept the loss, acceptance of yourself follows. I had four children to care for, and I needed to be whole in order to move on and succeed at motherhood and life itself. Accepting me was pivotal. Accept yourself, love yourself, know yourself, and honor yourself deep to the core of your being.

In order to truly love oneself, you must know yourself. The key for me during the final phase of my loss was "finding my center." It was imperative for living and carrying on that, I "find my center." When you find it, a love for self develops at a level beyond any understanding.

Finding your center to me means understanding yourself deep inside to your core. After this revelation and realization, anything is possible.

My success today correlates with my deep-rooted core values. Living my life driven from my core allows me to be true to myself, to my love for family, and love for professional leadership endeavors. Living and leading with a strong core means being clear about what you will accept, and what you will not accept. It means living a life to the fullest potential because all is done with purpose and with clear direction. Living with core values yields stability, security, happiness, and success.

They say change is strange, and this is so true. My loss caused a strange change that moved me through uncharted waters but navigating through the stages, and finally accepting, led to loving me and loving life. Moving through the stages, allowed for growth that enabled me to lead my children through uncharted territory without fear, and with a sense of strength, and self-worth that resulted in enhanced love, security, success, and joy.

Loss does not have to be the end for you, but the beginning of a new chapter. Allowing the process of grief to unfold, and moving through the necessary stages, will allow you to meet and greet your beautiful "inner core." Embrace it, for your happiness and success in life depends on truly loving yourself first. You must love the self first, before you can truly love another. You must know your inner self, so you can direct your future and navigate all that life has to offer.

Thank you for allowing me to share, Myrna.

THE POWER OF MEDITATION

I have read many books, and have seen many video tapes, and learned a lot about meditation. I practice meditation daily, and my words here come from my experiences. What I am about to write here to you, my reader, is my interpretation, as a person who loves to read and learn and practice those things that are going to bring my life to higher heights and deeper depths. I start my meditation in a quiet place, and I meditate indoors or outdoors alike. I love to go with a pad and a pen, in case, I want to jot down something, that I receive while meditating, which is so amazing that I need to write it down.

I make sure I am comfortable. I have loose and nice easy clothing on, I meditate with my eyes closed, and take some deep breaths, in and out, and this relaxes me. Breathing is soothing and calming. I allow my mind to just be. By that I mean, I don't force any thoughts, if they come, fine, if they don't come, just as fine. Meditation puts us with harmony, nature (if outdoors), gives us carefreeness, such joy and love. I notice after few minutes; I may have thoughts that float and words and meanings that are there. I follow the thought wherever it takes me, I travel with the thought. Sometimes it becomes a movie. At any point, if a negative thought enters my mind while in meditation, I immediately cast it out, and I breathe, and continue on. I meditate at times twenty to thirty minutes or even longer if it becomes so delicious, freeing, and so magical, I just want it to linger forever.

The purpose of meditation is to heighten your awareness, and it is to allow the mind and body to be at rest from people, places, and things, and it becomes just about you, and you alone. The peace you receive while meditating is supernatural. It is where you connect to Source, and it allows for you to enjoy a higher state of being, experiencing higher vibrations, and where thoughts become things. As I mentioned here, I release the negative thoughts, as in this state of being, you can create for yourself anything you want to do, or have, not only can you attract thoughts, but you can release what you don't want or need. Most people co-create, but you can also release, I do it all the time. Tell that thought, "Be gone."

Meditation is enjoying a feel-good state and in essence, silencing the world around you, in order to experience you, the inner you. It causes us to supernaturally become emotionally stable, as we conquer and find inner peace, tranquility, harmony, balance, and alignment with self. It is a highway to finding yourself and identity back, which we discussed in the beginning chapters. It is in this awakening that we experience that our thoughts matter, our inner voice matters, and receive the acknowledgment from Source, God, the Universe, your inner-being. It is so magical, that manifestations, of the thoughts you think, and you believe, and ask for, manifest. The problem that hinders our manifestations, is our belief, and our groaning and complaining. That is the biggest hindrance to your experiencing a manifestation-filled life. I've studied this enough and have come to the realization that in order to receive your miracle and your manifestation, you must be in a state of believing that you have already received it.

Funny how the Law of Attraction is so connected to the Word of God as in the Bible it states this in: Mark 11:24 (NKJV): "Therefore I say to you, whatever things you ask when you pray, believe that you receive them, and you will have them." In the Law of Attraction, your thoughts become things. However, the passage of Scripture says the same, whatever things you ask when you pray, (thoughts), (prayers), believe that you receive them, and you will have them. Same concept. The Universe is magical.

There is something said about the Bible, about the Law of Attraction. I took ahold of this, and I have seen it work in my life. I don't want to live my life in doubt, confusion, and have a poverty mindset, when I can have what I believe and think. Furthermore, the Bible states, clearly, that in Proverbs 23:7, "As a man thinks in his heart, so shall he be." Friends, it's what we think, bad or good thoughts, so shall we receive that thinking. It's either great thoughts, or stinking thinking. It's up to you, it is the Law of Attraction, and this law works. As I mentioned, what hinders those manifestations from coming into the natural realm of our lives, is our negative thinking that interrupts the process of the high vibrations you just created while meditating, and getting into the realm of receiving.

When I wrote here on living in the moment, I have been finding that living, truly alive, and well, and happy, and in the moment, receiving even those things you have not yet seen, you will receive them. But we hinder and block the process, the tunnel so to speak, with, soot and garbage, instead of freeing it, by say you want a house, and you block it by not even liking the house you live in, therefore already you have created a negative vibe, and therefore, the manifestation is hindered. Not gone, hindered, because as you again meditate, you get your mind in a state of quiet. Being in nature also brings us to a state of peace, and alignment with nature and self. Enjoying the butterfly, the flower, the trees, and the different colors of greens and the beautiful browns in the bark of the trees. This is nature, a gift given to us to enjoy and partake. Getting to my point, of nature and meditation, which is a different perspective, is that our lives are so busy, so in order to partake of being centered, in order to partake of being balanced, and being aligned, we must be quiet and be focused. Meditation does just that – it allows us to stop the train even for a little time in our daily history of this thing called life.

My desire for your life, as I share my learning experiences, in meditation, prayer, and being in nature, is for you to encounter self, self-worth, self-alignment, self-gratification. There is so much I learn in meditation, once I am done, I take my pad and pen and I make sure I write down all of the wonderful movies I just saw in my eyesight, all of my dreams, visions, and desires that I need to confess out loud. These thoughts, that I had in my meditation, I will make sure, I protect so that indeed they will come to fruition and come to pass. It is this closeness with self, via meditation, which brings closeness with self and true healing in your inner being. Don't block your manifestations by your negative beliefs. Change, purpose yourself to become a brand-new creation. How does stillness manifest your desires? It connects you to the details of who you are and makes explorations of your desires your potential. It connects you to your true power of you, therefore, to co-create with Source what you want out of life.

Experience the newness that comes from learning who your internal person is. Enough of what others say about you – what they think about you. That does not matter in the spectrum of this new majestic new life you are about to embark upon. This is a new day for you, especially if you have never meditated or co-created your life with Source. You will have the power and the anointing from God Almighty and the Universe and all his angelic beings will make sure you get your dreams to come true. You have the power and the authority to make your life the way you want it. No more how someone else wants it for you. You can move mountains just by speaking to the mountain. No longer are you the victim but you are now the victor. No longer are you the lost, but you are helping the lost. We have to be in the conquest of the knowledge of self, allowing time to simply be. Your destiny is here, I am giving you keys to progress in your growth, as you have been broken, damaged, hurt, it's time to take those old garments off and put on your robe of blessings. The new you is right here, right now. Take these steps of growth and don't look back.

"You need not leave your room, remain sitting at your table and listen. You need not even listen, simply wait. You need not even wait, just learn to become quiet, and still, and solitary. The world will freely offer itself to you to be unmasked. It has no choice; it will roll in ecstasy at your feet."

— FRANZ KAFKA, AUSTRALIAN PHILOSOPHER
AND POET

"Finally, brethren, whatever things are true, whatever things are noble, whatever things are just, whatever things are pure, whatever things are lovely, whatever things are of good report, if there is any virtue and if there is anything praiseworthy – meditate on these things."

— PHILIPPIANS 4:8, NKJV

SILENCE

In Silence I come to You,
Like a Deer panted
For Brooks of Water,
In the Morning Dew
Refresh my Thirsty Soul,
As I wait in Silence, for my Dove
I pierce my eyes with tears in love,
As you see me, from Up Above
In Silence, I now Become,
The One, who flies the skies above
My Arms are open for your Love,
I See you now, you are my Dove.

— MYRNA IVETTE
CLAUDIO

10

GIRL, STRAIGHTEN YOUR CROWN

Sometimes our crowns are a little crooked; girl, it's time to straighten your crown. Time to sharpen your tools, time to come to the realization that only you can change you. All the self-help books, and videos, and church, and coaches you get, can only get you to the place, where we are now. The time has come to make the decision to live your new life *now*. Time for changes to take effect, time to grow, time to flow, and time to stop procrastination, and letting others rule and reign your life and destiny. This is your life, no one else's; follow your instincts and your intuition, and take charge and take ahold of all you have learned herewith, and in other books, and in other ways. It's time to put our big girl pants on, straighten your crown, whether you are a man or a woman. We all have spiritual crowns, fix them, adjust them, center them, align them, and straighten them. This is your season, this is your calling, this is your destiny, the time is now, for you to experience your new life, a wonderful existence and experience. Make every day count. As Michelangelo painted his beautiful paintings, you can make your imaginary canvas and make every day a masterpiece. No more excuses, no more delays, no more hindrances, go out and do it, go out and get it, go out and live your life to the best of your ability, day by day, hour by hour, minute by minute, and second by second. Your destiny is here and now for the taking. Go and get it.

AN ANGEL NAMED PAT

I was walking through Macy's a while ago, when I noticed the most beautiful angel pendant on a woman, the sales lady, Lina, at one of the perfume counters. I gasped for air, and said, "Oh my, that is the most beautiful gold pendant of an angel I have ever seen." She said to me, "Only those that are meant to know my story will know it, and I will share it with you." I said to her, "I am writing a book in the future, regarding this subject matter of wellness and angels, relationships and healing." She said, "Good. Put it in your book." Her words were, "Put it in your book, I don't care." She reminded me of one of the wives of the movie *The Godfather*. She had this Brooklyn, Italian, kind of vibe about her.

She was sweet and nice, and at the same time street smart. She said that her Angel's name was Pat. She said to me, "I'm going to tell you my angel story," so I intently listened, as she told me that an angel appeared to her, and I just was drawn in. She told me that her husband lived his life as a bachelor, all the years they were married. She suffered long and refused give up on her marriage as she had children. It was important to Lina, that she stay in the marriage for her children's sake. "The more she stayed," she said, "the worse he got." She said, "I had it with him, and one night, while she was sleeping, she felt a kiss on the back of her head." She thought it was her daughter and son-in-law, who had just come home from being out that evening. When she opened her eyes, she saw an angel, and she said to me her angel's name was Pat.

She opened her eyes to see who kissed her. Before her eyes was the most beautiful creature of an angel that she had ever gazed her eyes on. The light shone so brightly; she was mesmerized. She described the angel that visited her, with long blond hair. She couldn't make out the face with the brightness of the being. She saw her hands, white garments, and a bright glow, so bright, her light hovered and covered her face. The angel now said to her, a few simple words, "Go on now," so clear, Lina knew it was time to leave. That is all she said, she then left the life of suffering, the man who betrayed over and over again, left him for good, and never looked back.

Lina said to me, she now wears that angel pendant so proudly, and those that will know her story will know that angels are real. She made a point for me to tell all in my book that her angel's name was Pat, and that angels are real. I promised her I would do that. I literally broke down in tears, I touched her angel pendant, and felt all that she was trying to tell all of us. In this beautiful story, she was not letting go, because she thought she was doing the right thing. That happened to me with Jeremy when I lived in the living room, that big space, with my mama Betty, as Jeremy continued to live his life as a single man, and yet being a married man. We were married for more than twenty-two years. I also did not want to get divorced, and have another broken relationship, for the children's sake, for the sake of being marked as yet having another divorce, I tried to hang in there also until I could not take it any longer. We both got the courage to leave and move forward into our destinies.

Nothing is ever written in stone, when there is hurt, abandonment, rejection, and abuse, we do not have to take that kind of life. You have to make choices, to be a survivor.

I am not telling anyone in this book to get divorced or separated, I am however telling you, that if you do, you will be okay, and that choice is yours and yours alone. Look at her story above, she needed angelic intervention in order for her to *go on now*.

It is the same situation when you are in association with certain individuals that bring you down, or do not treat you with respect. It doesn't only apply to you, your husband or wives, or your partner and mate. It could be a family member, or a friend, or colleague that takes advantage of your good nature. A lot of times, hurt people, hurt people because they get inferior, jealous of you, and in order to make themselves feel higher and better than you, they need to crush you down, so they build themselves up. This is a familiar spirit, which goes around hurting innocent people.

You can learn from the pages of this book, that you do not have to ever accept that kind of behavior, and it is imperative that you do not allow it, and you step away from those kinds of people that are not good for your well-being. Sometimes, you can hear this over and over, and know it is not good, then you are enabling this type of behavior and it will not get better, I know that for sure. It must cease, stop, and never happen in your life. It takes courage to leave people, places, things, and situations. But once you do, boy, you will walk away, smiling and proud, that you took the courage to put yourself first and foremost in the realm of your life, and left a possibly dangerous situation. You may think, you need all these friends, and folks, but what you really need are peace, and tranquility, and truly, you need you. In the previous chapter, I spoke on taking time for you and doing prayer and/ or meditation. It is key and it is time, for a new beginning for you.

POSITIVE AFFIRMATIONS

Positive affirmations are putting new seeds in the ground of something you've never had before. Practicing positive affirmations, words spoken out to the air, will create a whole new world for you. I, biblically, learned that, when they had no food in the Bible, Jesus said speak to the stones, and water gushed out. Sound creates healing; when you listen to the ocean or rain at night through the window, it's so peaceful, soothing, and healing. The stones apparently heard and broke and they drank water for days. Sound creates things, thoughts as we read create things, Jesus said, "Speak to the mountain (in your life), and it will go." When you go to an ultrasound and have kidney stones, they have ultra "sounds" to destroy the "stones." Interesting, that even science uses sound for healing. Speaking sounds out of our mouths, can also create healing for us. Positive affirmations create a belief that, when you do it with conviction, faith, and belief, that you know without a shadow of a doubt that it is so, it will be so. I am a firm believer in positive affirmations. In a previous chapter, we broke down some examples of speaking and turning the negative into a positive situation with our words. When God created the world, He did so in seven days, and spoke it out loud, "Let there be light," and it was so. Look below at these examples of positive affirmations.

EXAMPLES OF POSITIVE AFFIRMATIONS

- Today is a beautiful day, and all will go well for me
- I am thankful and grateful for my life
- I have money, and my bank account is full of money
- I am happy, healthy, wealthy, and wise

- Today is the beginning of the greatest days ahead
- I am successful in all I try to do and achieve
- Today I will not judge anyone but will keep myself flowing in good attitudes
- My gifts and creativity are growing daily in my life
- Amazing doors of success keep opening up for me
- All my bills are paid, and I am always living in abundance
- I love my life, I am free, I am strong, and I am focused
- People that are negative will not affect me; I will move on in joy
- I will own the house that I've dreamed of
- Today I desire to grow and have the life I have always dreamed of

These are just a few examples that I put here, but you can use these or make up your affirmations as you are home, or driving, or even taking a walk. Update them weekly or when you feel like it, as you go along. These affirmations are key in my life and I make it a habit to change them as I desire, and I get bold with them, and I decree, declare, and believe with all of my being that just like God, as I am made in His likeness and image, just like He created the worlds by the words He spoke, that I too, can create my world by the words I speak. It is my world that I am creating when I do positive affirmations, and get creative, they can be quite fun. Today, is the first day of the rest of your life, time to leave the past behind, to not stress about the future, to live in the moment, and to be the free beautiful spirit you were created to be. Today, make your world a new creating, go ahead, go on now.

MIRROR LOVE

This is an exercise that will go deep into your inner child, and bring inner healing, especially if there was a lack of love around you when you were growing up; even if you experienced love as a child, this is still an awesome exercise to do. It is an intimate exercise. At first, I felt ridiculous, dumb, and silly, but then I did it, such a simple thing, and the more I did it, the more comfortable I felt, and yet many will not do it. It goes like this: you stand and you look in the mirror, and you say three simple words to yourself, to your soul, to your inner-being, to your inner child, you say *I love you, I love you,* and repeat again and again, until you feel to stop, *I love you.* You will know when to stop; do it until you feel you are done. Remember, whatever you see inside of you, is exactly what you are dealing with, and know that this is a mirror only reflection, of what is truly inside of you. Begin to tell it, I love you.

Well, the first time, I did this exercise, I cried like a baby, it really brings inner healing. I have read this in few books, I also saw a YouTube video with Louise Hay, telling people to do this exercise. Let me tell you, it works, it really does. Now, I do not do this daily. When I do it is only spontaneously, if am just coming out of the bathroom say, I see myself, in the mirror, and it reminds me to tell myself, *I love you.* I stare in the mirror, and it's not easy for some people to do this, as they have deep wounds inside of their hearts, but I look at myself, and say at least three times, "I love you, I love you, I love you!" This affirms your love for yourself, and the fact that you are seeing your face, and looking into your soul, there is much healing in this exercise. I only do it, as I feel the need to do it. However, I do my meditation, or positive affirmations, daily, but it really is a nice exercise of self-healing and love for yourself. Now, when I do it, I take pride in it, and do it with joy; the tears are not there, or maybe they will come again, we have to flow in the spirit, we are not married to the same events and feelings in our lives. We evolve and change and grow. Please take note of this one exercise as it really frees your inner child. Keep in mind that love is not a feeling, a feeling is an emotion that changes; love is a commitment to love someone deeply and it's a beautiful and amazing gift.

When you take ahold of your growth seriously, and vigorously, it's like going to the gym. When you work out, you see a change, here and there, you say, "Oh my, I lost inches, and look better in this part of my body," and little by little you see changes. It is the same with your spiritual growth, and your inner healing. You grow and see changes, you're not affected as much by what others say or do, or don't do. Rejections, abandonments, and those emotions we broke down in the beginning of the book just don't seem to take effect or take ahold and grasp at your heart strings anymore. You flow with the winds and waves of the oceans. You become like the wind – now you see me, now you don't – you experience life in another level of intimacy for yourself. All of these things, that I have spoken about in these chapters, have now brought you a new wave, a new light, a new way of living and thinking. You are making deposits – like into the bank – into your spirit being, deposits that will carry you through life: positive affirmations, and positive thinking, and creating your world by the way you think.

JOURNAL DAILY

It is important that you realize that the blessing is in the journey, not the destination. The destination can take a little time, what are you going to do – be miserable until you get your blessing, your answer, your manifestation? It is in the road trip that you are taking and the truck stops, and the food, and the places you stop at to take pictures – a good way to look at it – not in the destination. The destination is the peak, yes, but are you going to groan and complain because you are still waiting for an answer to your prayer? Things get delayed for a reason: you, this, that, and this other.

It doesn't matter, what matters is right now is: are you living the life that will get you the life you want? If you complain, you are blocking the avenue and bringing a negative force into the positive vibe, that you already are believing for.

Another way for growth is journaling. Journaling keeps track of all of our growth in progress. It is a beautiful way to take away any stress, and writing a journal brings a sense of gratification, of all you have done, are doing, and planning to do. You can journal your short-term and long-term goals in there as well. I name my journals by number – one, two, three – and I date when I start each journal pad to when I finish, then start a new one. The other day, I picked up a journal of prayers I prayed, and every single one was answered. Same would have been if I meditated, the answers came. This journal was about three years old.

It was pretty nice seeing that, and that made me happy to continue to journal my life and progress, as I grow to become a better person. A person who feels they have arrived has already lost, because we never arrive, because we as humans keep evolving, growing from higher heights to deeper depths. We go from spirit to spirit, and from glory to glory. Infinity does not have an end. Sometimes, I have procrastinated, and journaled that I procrastinated; it was like a mirror of what I do, so I don't want to keep writing that, so I change for the better. I grow and move forward in the goals I have journaled and created for myself. Keep growing, achieving, and moving forward, soldier of life.

A nice exercise while journaling: in your daily journaling, you can make a list of positive aspects you want to achieve, how to make ways for you to go out and enjoy your days and find subjects and avenues of good feelings and emotions. Write down subjects that would bring good feelings and emotions and what makes you happy. Go further and write what makes your heart beat, and thrilled, and happy. Write down your downfalls, and also your dreams. This makes you even appreciate others more, you can love more, forgive easier.

But how, can I be 100 percent? By just believing even for one minute you are 100 percent, you already are. It's not great invention, no great tasks, just daily growth, and love medicine for your inner-being, who's inside of you saying I'm ready to love again, I'm ready to fly, I'm ready to do that which I am born to do. We need to believe is the key, and to have vitality for life-giving potential. You have potential and it was buried. Now it is a tree growing and birds are perching in your branches.

DENOUNCE THE NEGATIVE

Denounce the negative that would try to creep in, so I speak out loud, get away from me, negative words, thoughts, vows, or curses. Take ahold of your destiny. The time is now, not tomorrow, but now. Draw from within yourself the love you need. You have the ability, and stability now to go forward. You have love, mercy, and grace following you all the days of your life. You have now more determination than ever before, you have peace, love, and joy. It's becoming more and more evident that you are a butterfly changed from a caterpillar. You need to be persistent in your denouncing, determined, disciplined, decisive, have direction, and be firm in your dos and don'ts, and make right choices and decisions that will align with your spirit.

TIME TO STRAIGHTEN YOUR CROWN

It is time to straighten your crown. You know time flies, and this is not time for going backward, but it's time to move ahead, to be mindful of who you are, and whose you are, because you are God's creation. You are a queen, an eagle, a butterfly. Stay focused, and allow others to fly, and let them make their own mistakes. You are not responsible for anyone's destiny. We are given the responsibility of our consciousness. Be about your business, be strong, live well, be happy, love humanity. In this, all of the brokenness you have experienced, will fade away to nothing, it will be as silk, as you live in the land of milk and honey.

"Love suffers long and is kind; love does not envy; love does not parade itself, is not puffed up; does not behave rudely, does not seek its own, is not provoked, thinks no evil; does not rejoice in iniquity, but rejoices in the truth; bears all things, believes all things, hopes all things, endures all things. Love never fails."

—1 CORINTHIANS 13:4 TO 8, NKJV

QUEEN OF AGES

Queen of Ages,
There I Stand
Looking Gorgeous,
From a Glance
I see your Love,
From Within
That Men Destroyed,
And Now You Win
Are you My King,
The One I Hear
Yes, do not Fret,
My Reina Dear
When Winds turn turmoil,
The Oceans Rage
Know that Am Here,
Your Ancient of Days

— I.E., (G_D) MYRNA IVETTE
CLAUDIO

11

THE DOOR TO YOUR DESTINY AWAITS

Now that you are coming along nicely in your healing process, the little devil on your shoulder will try to tell you to go back to the way it was. Go ahead – feel rejected, feel abandoned, feel left out – let me tell you, you have come a long way baby, don't allow the little foxes to spoil your vine. Your vine, your trees, your crops have begun to prosper and here come the little foxes, trying to bring you down. Rise up from that field and get your pesticide spray and spray them out of your field. You no longer have to take anything from anyone, ever again. You are royalty, which is the way it works, you need to see yourself as the King or the Queen of your existence and your kingdom. Let nothing or no one steal from your crops, steal your wellbeing, or your joy. You've worked too hard, and come too far, to let anything ever again stand in your way. Move over foxes, it's my time. We are meant in the Word of God to be royal priesthoods and holy nations. You are a nation, your own government, you own your kingdom, and as soon as you get ahold of a bad experience, grab ahold of it and tell it where to go. Take authority once and for all – for the door to your destiny awaits.

At this point in my journey, I am already living my newfound life, and learning to progress with healing from the broken relationships that I encountered. In this chapter, I want to reinforce and encourage you to not give up, and not to give in, to continuing to live a life of pain and suffering. It is imperative that we learn to know when to say yes, and when to say no. Saying yes for pleasing others is extremely dangerous. Many times, we stay in situations like I did, with Jeremy. It was doable for the time, as I was there with my children, because in my case, as I had written previously, he never came home, but just to sleep, so in a way, I was accustomed to him already not being there, and I was already in a separated state. My fear of leaving created the questions that went through my head, like where would I go, how can I do this financially? I had many questions going through my head, as I wanted to just leave. I opted to stay, and as you know, there came a time, when you know that it's time to move on. The same thing happened to Lena, with her not wanting to leave because of her children, that she received angelic intervention.

LET YOUR YES BE YES, AND YOUR NO BE NO

Many times, we tend to be yes people, when we are insecure, not healed, and dependent on others to live our lives. They call that being a "yes" person. We say yes to everything, in order to have acceptance from others. Afraid they no longer will like us, or even include us in their lives. Yes this, yes that. It is important we stop the pattern of saying yes, especially when you really mean no. Once you take your authority, as a human being, you throw those noes out of your mouth, with no second thoughts. Your yes will be real. Your noes will free you. You do not have to say yes to everything in order to be accepted. Once you accept yourself, just for who you are, you stop being a people pleaser. It is driven out of fear of being rejected. Why is this so important in this stage of the process? It is important, because we have to become decisive people, people of worth, people that are defined by our character, for what we stand for, saying what we mean, and meaning what we say. Many people read books to help themselves but go on with life and never change. I truly encourage you to take the steps laid out in this book, with bullet points and all.

EMPHASIZING STEPS

It is important that you go over all the emotions that we all feel, when we experience a loss, or such as broken relationships. As you already read, they are insecurities, rejection, abandonment, fears, unforgiveness, to mention some of the key emotions we went over in detail. I want to point out that I broke down the definition of these emotions clearly, so you are keen and aware, of what you are experiencing, which emotion and when.

The steps to take for growth – such as having gratitude, thankfulness, prayer, meditation, positive affirmations – have all been clearly defined the middle chapters as well. We broke down the emotions, then, the steps to take. It is not only important, but imperative, that we actively start the process laid out in the pages of this book. In order to live the life you have been searching for, it takes a revolution, a changed mindset, a want to change, in order to realize those potentials that are already inside of your being. You carry the seed of potentiality. You were born this way.

THE DOOR TO YOUR DESTINY AWAITS

This is not the time to give in. Destiny had you read this book. I believe in destiny. I believe the Universe and all the galaxies, stars, and angels brought you to this point of decision, and you were aligned to read it. Are you going to follow the crowd, the crowd that goes on the main street, or are you going to take the steps in this book, and pursue your destiny that's awaiting? Are you going to open door number one, where you will follow the crowd and stay the same? Or, are you going to open door number two, which has you thinking and pondering about it, and in the end you will do nothing with the words I've written for you, and you end up the same, and possibly, end up with another abusive relationship, or heartbreak? Or will you open door number three, the door to your destiny, and as you open it, there will be the real "yes," and you will be answered by the gift of potentiality, and revelation that you've never encountered before. Door number three will bring about all the knowledge, all the increase, all the change, all the blessings, all the miracles' signs and wonders. The answer is in you, in door number three. Do not stay frozen in time, and end up the same. Open the right door, and be the person that from this day forward, cannot be stopped, cannot be messed with, and will be the queen of her dynasty and destiny. The choice is yours. Which door will you walk through?

THE POWER OF YES

Once you commit and say yes to your new life, it's time to take ahold the reins of your life and become the determined person you have always wanted to be. Time to get to the store and get yourself a beautiful journal for your words of life to be written upon. It is time to organize yourself and make your first list of priorities. It is time to access your spot of peace, where you will be comfortable to pray or do meditation. Make a list of places you can go that you know are quiet and peaceful, where it would be great for nature encounters, and quiet times of reflection. I am so excited for you, as you now venture into your newfound life of freedom and joy to be experienced by you, and you, alone. Being alone is a gift in itself, being with people is also. But when you are alone, you can gather your thoughts, and make sense of life. It's that sweet, it's that simple.

It is so exciting, as I share this new life with you, that it makes me want to get up tomorrow morning and refresh my goals. One of the key components is setting goals, first, short-term and also long-term. Take time for yourself to do this small and easy task. You will thank yourself when you see them coming to pass. Reward yourself each and every time you meet your goals. Start with as little as a six-month set of goals, then one year, and up to even three to five years. Or just start small with up to a year, that is fine; there are no rules here in this thing called life.

The most important thing is you work daily on achieving spiritual growth and success. Walking is something I do on a regular basis, I walk sometimes even just thirty minutes a day. I listen to tapes. I love listening to Abraham Hicks, and/ or Louise Hay, I get so encouraged by them, via YouTube. I'm being real, as to what I do. I also love to take time for prayer, daily, and sometimes, I am not perfect, I miss a day, and guess what, I do not beat myself up for it. I do what I can, as I go along my journey. Remember, you are not married to anything that I am saying or that I've written – this is a guide to bring you closer to the person you were born to become. One of the things that I always say, I am a work in progress, and guess what, I always will be a work in progress, but I promise, each day will get better and better. You may have days that you just want to chill and relax, just do nothing but rest. That is fabulous, that is your body telling you to do that, and you, being all full of wisdom, not beating yourself up about it, is the reward. Take time for you, to enjoy even those times of pure nothing, and just resting. It's a beautiful thing.

PROCRASTINATION

Now, I've gone all happy and ready to rock and roll, but the spirit of procrastination creeps in. Happens to the best of us. One day, okay, two maybe, but if you are stuck like a couch potato, going on more than a week, that's not going to help you come to the place that you are destined to go. Procrastination is the action of delaying or postponing something. I want you, at this point, to be aware that this is something that happens to people that stunts their inner healing and growth. You have the power within you to rise up, get up, and get going. It is just a matter of faith, and a matter of making the decision to go forward. I will, however, say if you find yourself alone, and this goes on longer than expected, you may want to reach out to someone you trust for help and to talk things over with them. I myself had over the phone sessions of therapy, which were beneficial to me in my life. That is only a choice that each individual makes, and no one can make it for you. Only you would know, what is required in your life.

MAKING TIME FOR YOU

Another hindrance that stops us from growing is time. We are too busy. We work all day, and cook, and clean. It seems there's just not enough time to pursue the process laid out in this book, because my life is so busy. I say this: there's always time when it comes to you. You make time happen. It's called time management, managing and organizing your time around the most important person in the planet, which is you, my friend. There is no excuse that is big enough when it comes to your well-being. Life is going to continue moving on, the earth will continue to rotate on its axis. "The Earth's axis runs from the North Pole to the South Pole. It takes the Earth twenty-four hours, or one day, to make one complete rotation around this invisible line. As the Earth rotates, each area of its surface gets a turn to face and be warmed by the sun. This is important to all life on Earth," according to an article in National Geographic Society and Science: Solar System.

Beloved, you have twenty-four hours a day, to make something happen. You need to say to yourself, "I'm about to make something happen." There is no time, on this green earth, for procrastination, for being a yes person, for allowing people to step all over you, and for the lies and deceptions you have learned to live with, and for abusive relationships. It's high time to learn a new way, a new path, a new process. Make time for you – you are worth it.

LOT'S WIFE FROZE

There was a story in the Bible of Lot's wife. Everything fell to pieces, and the Bible says, in Genesis 19:24, "The Lord rained brimstone and fire on Sodom and Gomorrah, from the Lord out of the heavens," so in Genesis 19:26: "But Lot's wife looked back behind him, and she became a pillar of salt." So, they all ran, except for her, she stood there and looked back, and the Bible says, she froze. She froze in time, she never went forward, she froze, and stayed in her past, she never entered her future, she stood, and therefore, she froze. A great lesson in this is to not live in your past and keep looking back. Don't be like Lot's wife, move out of your past, move into your future, get out of your head, and we all have stinking thinking, get out of your way, stop hindering your growth, and allow yourself the opportunity to take chances to grow, to be a better person.

When reading this, whether you are a young woman, an older woman, a young man, an older man, it doesn't matter – the only thing that matter is not age, it's not stature, it's us, it's our own sometimes even rebellion, laziness, or even a spirit of procrastination, I just don't care attitude. That is fine, many people will not desire to come closer to being the raw people that they need to get to be. Like they say with the onion, it stinks growing; you can need to be willing to experience growing pains, but in the end, it will all be worth it.

I'm not calling anyone rebellious or lazy, I am directing that directly to the spirit behind the scenes, which causes some of us a hindrance in our growth and potential. Myles Monroe wrote a book once, I cannot recall the name, I read it a long time ago, and he said, our potential is more in the cemeteries than in the living. Books never written, movies never produced, doctors, lawyers, teachers, never graduated, and so on, and so on, he said, there is more potential in the cemetery than on this earth. You do not want to be a statistic, where all your dreams and visions will die there. Rise up, Lazarus, life is for the living, and get your dream fulfilled, even if it is just to get to the beach. The dream does not matter in equivalency – what matters is that you fulfill it.

Do not allow anyone ever again to steal your joy. I remember, being a baby Christian and there was a Revivalist in town. I went, excited, I wanted to experience an old time religion revival. The preacher came over to me and said, "You are getting a new joy, it will be a joy unspeakable, without measure, that no man can take away." Amazingly, I was beyond happy that this revival preacher came to me and said, "God said to tell you," and those were the words, which came out of his mouth. Let me tell you, I believe that I will never forget those words. We can experience this in our lives, it does not have to be just me. We can all say to ourselves, in one of our positive affirmations, Myrna, I have a new joy; it is a joy unspeakable, without measure, that no man can take away. Imagine saying those words to yourself, every now and then.

IT'S GOING TO TAKE FAITH

Faith is the evidence of the thing you hope for, but you don't see. It takes faith to move a mountain. It takes faith, to believe for healing, it takes faith to believe for restoration in relationships and people's lives. It's going to take a blind faith, to believe that you can have all that you believe. You can achieve that which you do not see in the natural realm of things. Faith is a power that comes from believing that which is in the invisible realm. It is not just believing, but you can let it even grow deeper and have the kind of faith which is wrought out of nothing. Faith carries people from one place of existence into another. Faith is living in the natural world, but believing in the supernatural world. When you go into this deep, intense belief that no matter what, you will achieve that which you have set your mind to believe, then you win. Faith brings the supernatural into the natural world. In order to achieve the manifested success of answered prayers and manifestations that you have asked for, you must first listen carefully. I already told that you are in a natural world, and you must step into the supernatural world to bring it forth.

Here it is: you not only need to step into the supernatural, but you must abide there and live a supernatural life, to regularly see supernatural miracles. Miracles and manifestations are not natural. They come from another world, another realm, the Universe, so you must step into the supernatural, abide there, stay, and ponder in meditation and prayer that keeps you there, for as long as you want to be there. You need to pull down to the natural earthly realm – you need to pull down the supernatural, where miracles abide.

Therefore, friends, abide in the supernatural realm of the impossibilities. You can do it. I don't want to be in the natural, I want to live a supernatural existence. I want to be where miracles abide. Abide in a supernatural world, and pull those manifestations down to the natural realm. Explore, abide, and go there – there is majesty awaiting at your feet. All the angels, galaxies, Universe, God, your inner-being are all awaiting at your beck and call. They want to serve you and give you more that you ever could have imagined you can do, or achieve. Once you have tasted of the gifts of life, the fruits of the spirit, and the brightest colors of the rainbow, you will always want to dine there.

Step now into the river of life, and don't look back like Lot's wife. Daily pursue happiness. You deserve to be happy, and if someone told you in the past you don't deserve anything, I am here to change that confession and tell you do deserve to be happy. Happiness is a temporary event, because the root of the word happiness, is rooted in happenings, so when something happens, you then are happy. You're happy when events make you happy, because something caused you to be happy. But when you have "unspeakable joy," no man and no happenings can take that away from you. Be happy, be joyful, rejoice in your new beginnings. Do not allow the enemy to steal the fruit of your vine. Do not allow the enemy – that's anything or anybody – to steal your joy, and do not allow anything or anybody to take what you have planted and eat the crops that you have worked so hard to plant and produce.

Be alert, be vigilant, for the enemy is like a roaring lion seeking whom he may devour. Good news, if you're rooted in a strong field, of good soil, the enemy cannot steal anything. You need to be rooted and grounded in love, and in knowing who you are. Listen, this is true, and this is good: if you don't know who you are, then guess what, someone else will tell you who you are, and you do not want that. You must know who you are, and by following the steps I laid out – of meditation, positive affirmations, and learning to grow in ways to help your well-being – you will know who you are, and whose you are. Keep in mind – obstacles come and go but you must be an overcomer, and step over every one of them.

"Now faith is the substance of things hoped for, the evidence of things not seen."

— HEBREWS 11:1, NKJV

COUNTRY GIRL ARISING

In dedication to my ideal reader.

We fall in love, sometimes, too quick, but you outsmart us, coz you got wit, then suddenly the truth sets in, and I do feel bad, we women know this trick. We're grown up little girls, putting our boots and lipstick on, with mascara running down our faces, and yet we still keep dancing, but we've hidden the hurt beyond measure, betrayed, and then, alone. now moving forward, on to higher heights, and deeper depths, hoping this time, we win, no mountain can stop this country girl arising.

— MYRNA IVETTE CLAUDIO

12

LOVE AWAKENING – MY KNIGHT IN SHINING ARMOR

This is a revolution of life, a great awakening, a great revival. When you come to realize the awakening experience that you are now living, nothing or no one can steal your joy away. That is called a great awakening or a love awakening. Love is the most powerful entity in the entire universe. With love, people have moved mountains, have climbed the to the highest peaks, and ventured into great seas. It is time to set up new goals: short-term goals and long-term goals. It is imperative that you face your fears, that you are bold, that you are strong, and take life by the horns.

Always remember, the love of self is the greatest love awakening and why? It is because, if you love yourself, you can then understand how to love another. In this book, you have read that it is not just your time, it is your turn. You have come to a clear understanding of self-love, and self-gratification, and have learned how to achieve a successful plan for your new bright future. I'm happy that as you read these words, your heart will capture like a camera the great insights in these pages of creating a new life for yourself, and I'm not just saying you will, but you really will. We cover here the love of self, your true north and North Star, that we can in fact, love again, meditation, and positive affirmations. The day is here for your great awakening, the revolution of your newfound life, and your true inner revival.

CELINE DUG'AL ROUSSEAU'S STORY

I was already being ordained as an evangelist, and had started the work of counseling. We then became best of friends, and still are. Celine DuG'al Rousseau, a thirty-two-year-old woman, was married to David for nine years, when all hell broke loose. Celine had been having problems with the family, the mother-in-law, and sister-in-law; this did not help her marriage in any way shape or form. David was a musician by night, and a car mechanic by day. He was a functional working alcoholic, with an overbearing mother, and a wicked, in her words, sister-in-law.

In Celine's words: knowing this after I married him, I just knew I had no shot at all. I had my son at twenty-seven years old, and I had the marriage, the house with the white picket fence, that almost turned blood red, the works, I had the world ahead of me. We bought our house, we both worked, and had a DJ Business on the side making six grand a month. We are doing well for ourselves. All is going well, when one evening, David and I had plans to go out, but before going out, he disappears, I waited a few hours, and took my car and went looking for him, I saw the Bar and Grille and went to the back to park, and as I pulled up into the parking lot, there was our family van. I then see this woman, open the van door, and take out my son's car seat, and throws it into the back of the van, of course, I am not stupid, I knew it was to make room for her and my husband to spend time together and to do the unspeakable.

I quickly parked, and I came out of nowhere, like a bat

out of hell, and I lost it. I saw fire red; this has never happened to me and now this woman is in front of me. I grabbed her by the hair and pushed her downward, she was screaming, I am married, and kept showing me her wedding finger and wedding ring. I immediately grabbed my van keys out of her hand. I flew into the bar and proceeded toward my husband, he never saw me coming, I came like a bow and arrow to its target, or like a bull in a china shop, ready to confront him. As I dodged toward him, he was profusely drunk, I punched him in the face, and he fell off his chair. Yes, I did. He got up and said to me, he told me to go home.

I had a sense something was up, as I had seen my van around the corner parked, several times, but I thought he was working, as he did side jobs. I already had a sense he was cheating on me, and now it was confirmed. This all stemmed from his mother and sisters' dislike for me. Especially his sister who kept on antagonizing and meddling in our marriage.

At this point, my son was two years old, and now I felt all different kinds of emotions, I felt anger, rage, abandonment, fear, unforgiveness, rejection, fear, betrayal, mistrust, scared, and lonely. I prayed, I didn't know where to go, who to talk to and I sensed to go to church on Sunday and see if I can get prayer. After several weeks of going to several services, I liked it and kept on attending. As I am walking through the lobby doors into the sanctuary of the church, on a Sunday morning service, there she is: Myrna. We met for the first time. She said, "Hi, I've seen you here, a few times. How are you?" I briefly told her what I had recently encountered, she said to me, "After church, let's get lunch across the street at the diner." We did, and I shared with her my recent events.

Celine's story touched me, so I offered her my counseling services, and we began to meet for her sessions. I pointed out the biggest problems, and I laid out the steps I would teach her. I began by identifying the emotions she was dealing with that kept surfacing on a daily basis. I taught her ways to combat these emotions and tackle them strategically. I set up with her short- and long-term goals. We met consistently for a period of over six months.

We decided to go to dinner when Celine tells me that David, her husband, filed for divorce as he found another woman. Imagine at this juncture how she must have been feeling. She left the home a year later as things were getting more and more difficult, and yet she was feeling stronger, and the counseling sessions were helping her. She stated that she was emotionally stronger and felt happy to be moving on with her life. She and I became friends after her counseling sessions, and she was a whole other woman. She was socializing, she was in church helping others hurting, God was using her, and I was elated and amazed at her progress.

She was getting ready to leave and shared she had no place to go. This is my friend, who I've known for years, not just counseled, so I asked her if she would like to stay with me and my family until she finds a place. She did. We had so many great memories. We went to church together, we laughed, her son was playing with my sons. It was a special time for all of us.

Celine's state of being and wellbeing was amazing. She went out and got a nice job at a car dealership, she was social, happy, strong-minded, she went to social events, church gatherings, and she really allowed her past to stay in her past. Her main concern was her son, and he was doing well, with friends, and in school. She no longer was dealing with those emotions, of fear, abandonment, rejection, loneliness, and she has grown to be a strong woman, mother, and always a wonderful being and friend. She moved out and found a nice place to live, and for years, she worked, and continued thriving in her new life.

Love does come around, as a light, and it shows up for her, and she is elated. She met a wonderful man, Michael, who showed her love, love for her son, and is a caring person.

They have been married now for twenty-two years. She shared with me that he is a stand-up man – she calls him her big teddy bear – who loves working out and he works out daily, a muscle man, who loves spending time in the gym. Today, they both attend a local church regularly where her husband is the drummer in the church band.

Celine is a beautiful woman, who loves with all her heart, and gives all that she is to whoever needs it. She went through much suffering in her previous marriage, and was able to come out of it, and is now happily married, and her son, as well, is doing well. I am so happy we met, and I was able to counsel her and help her, and most importantly, we are friends for life. Thank you, Celine, for sharing this story with me, as I write it in the pages of this book, knowing that it will help many who are suffering from breakups and divorce, infidelity, and emotional heartache. Your story is going to bring hope and healing to many, thank you.

In life, we must find our equilibrium. A balance, the center of our being, and an alignment are good ways to describe what we need in order to not just understand life, but to understand your true north, being you. In the pages of this book, I have laid out the hurts, feelings, and emotions that a person can encounter in a loss, such as a death of a loved one, a breakup, a divorce, or even the loss of a good friend. When we encounter these emotions of grieving and loss, we can experience a myriad of emotions. In recapping this last chapter of the book, we already broke down in detail the emotions that we can encounter with those life experiences.

We discussed in detail the emotion of insecurity, the mother of all emotions and why it is. We discussed abandonment, fears, unforgiveness, rejection, and emotions that can bring a person, if not dealt with, to depression and other outcomes from such damaged emotions. It is imperative that we learn to know how we feel. If don't examine these hurts inside of us, we can continue, of course, to live the life we have been living. For example, if I didn't want to be healed, and leave the relationship, in order to have my self-preservation, I could have, and I truly believe this, I could have gone into a depression. You must hit rock bottom, before you realize the severity of your situation. I pray you catch that ball, even before it hits the ground.

It is better to be at a 100 percent wholeness, than at a 50 percent half wholeness. I said that when two individuals enter a relationship half-healed, you do not become 100 percent together. You are still broken. That mentality, if not correct, is my assumption that a whole and a whole makes a wonderful thing. A half and a half create two people trying to feed off each other without, listen carefully, being whole. You can heal while single, or being in a relationship; it's the work you have to put into yourself. Many people put the work into their bodies, always at the gym, always taking care of their outside appearance, and even taking care of others. However, they lack the importance of knowing that unless you take care of yourself first, you can never take care of another. Yes, you can take care of another person, and be not healed, but what I am projecting here is that the dimension of your love and care for another, will be that much greater in knowledge and power. The reason being is that once you can truly love yourself, you can truly love another better.

A ROSE FOR YOU

The red rose symbolizes romance, love, beauty, and courage. A red rosebud signifies beauty and purity. A thornless red rose means love at first sight. Yellow roses symbolize friendship and joy, and new beginnings. Orange roses symbolize fascination, desire, and sensuality.

Roses are red, violets are blue, true love awaits, and it's all for you. Flowers are beautiful in their essence and glory, and the rain supplies the water they need, and the sun makes them shine brightly on a sunny day. Incredibly fascinating to me how the roses in different colors do have more than one meaning. For instance, in the case of a red rose, it is not just about romance and love, it signifies beauty – your beauty, your essence, who you are – and if you feel that beauty, don't wait to get a romantic red rose, buy yourself one. A red rose signifies courage; this is so beautiful to me. Look at the yellow rose, it's not just for friendships, it also symbolizes joy, and new beginning. Celebrate with a yellow rose when starting these new beginnings. There are several meanings, and I love the ones that correlate to us as individuals and not only necessarily for just romance giving. You are a rose, in a garden of love, you deserve to be watered with love and showers of joy. Practice that love for yourself. Smile at the little things, for no reason at all; laugh – it's good medicine for all of us.

WHERE DOES THE WIND BLOW

Enjoy the winds of time. If you want to go here, go here; if you want to go there, just go there; go as the winds come and go, and flow so you can feel the wind beneath your feet. The winds do not know when they are coming or going. Be like the wind – live your life full of joy and freedom. In the middle section of this book, I laid out steps to becoming that free person who lives and moves with the winds of time. Be true to yourself, be raw at times, there is beauty in being real and raw; it's called transparency. It is then, that the freshness of your being is exposed in order be healed. Allow the healing process to bring you to the place of victory. Allow the winds of time to carry you forward into your destiny. I encourage you to stop looking back. There is nothing back there – it only hinders your movement forward.

YOUR TRUE NORTH

True north is the direction that points directly toward the geographic North Pole. This is a field point on the Earth's globe. Why do people say true north? A compass provides the ideal metaphor. Just as compass points toward a magnetic field, your "true north" directs your path and pulls you forward.

Metaphorically speaking, it is to move you forward. It is intended to be a guidance in our lives. I wear a true north pendant every day of my life. If I take off for some reason, I put it back on. I just love the northern lights, and the northern star, to me its meaning is symbolic, for the North Star depicts a beacon of inspiration and hope to many.

Whether you follow the stars, or your true north, the spark of imagination from which visions and dreams come from, they come from a place of hope, light, love, and possibilities of amazing wonders. The message here is go forward, don't look back, don't be like Lot's wife in the Bible, and freeze in your past. The horizon you look to is full of unlimited potential. Do not allow your hopes and dreams to be buried in the cemetery with unfulfilled potential. Like I said, take the trip, buy the shoes, take the course, write the book – you have the power within you to make your dreams come true and your visions a reality. I encourage you to take the steps and start your journey of using these benefits. If you do not try these benefits, you will never know the priceless miracles, signs, and wonders that await you on the horizon.

Here I will tell you, that after I left Jeremy, and moved on, I mentioned that I got an apartment, landed a nice job, I was settled and started to find myself back, found my identity back as I experienced a beautiful joy. However, after being alone for several years, I decided I would date once again. At this point, I was not at the 100 percent level I mentioned, but I was doing well emotionally, feeling stronger and stronger by the day. I must have been feeling in the scale of about a good 80 to 85 percent emotionally better. I began dating, and did go on several dates, and nothing was making me feel excited about anyone. Dating is not easy, but I pursued the dating game.

MY KNIGHT IN SHINING ARMOR: IN MEMORY OF JULIO CESAR PARDO (R.I.P)

I finally met Julio, he was from Colombia, and a proud United States citizen, as he lived many years in Wisconsin, twenty-five years to be exact. He was also divorced. He was tall, dark, and handsome, and a Latino like me. He loved to dance, just like me. We laughed all the time, we danced, we traveled extensively. I took him to my island of Puerto Rico, and he fell in love with the island, he said, "We are going to retire here, honey." He was hard-working man with a nice job, and I had my job, we were happy, and we clicked. One of the most amazing things is the love my children have for Julio. They share the love of football, and family gatherings. He is what a woman would want in a stepfather for her children. I tell this part of my story, to tell you that during all of the pain, you can be happy and find love again. Amid the storms, in life, there is a light that dawns in the morning, a great new awakening.

I am going to be raw honest with you, Julio's demeanor, extremely beautiful inside and out, he was like a gift from heaven, but no man is perfect, but was raw and humble, and the kindest man. He was not perfect by any means, he was moody at times, and had little boy tantrums, but would get over them soon. All in all, I finally felt safe, secure, and blessed. I said to myself, "How did I get so lucky and blessed?" My security did not come from having a man; it came from my healing, that I had worked on for so long. It was the also the fact that I did not settle and did not waiver. I stood my ground and believed in him, my knight in shining armor, and he came forth as my new dawn in the morning dew. True love is real when you see yourself in your partner. We did not marry, but we recently got engaged. Julio gave me a beautiful engagement ring, so I became his fiancée when he asked me to marry him. I was elated, working, living my best life. We also had a dog, a Frenchie Bull Dog, named Lola, also known as Lolita. She was the life of the party and the love of Julio for sure.

Some say, especially because they have been hurt, whether the man hurts the woman, or the woman hurts the man, that they give up on trying to find the right person that makes you happy. Give love a chance, and never give up, dreams do come true. Some people try and try to have a baby, never give up, whether you try different avenues or adopt, there is always a way, where there seems to be no way. Julio and I, not the perfect couple, for no one is perfect, we however, always put each other first. My true love, how I love you, words cannot describe the love I have for you.

We were now seeing each other, for several years and so happy, and here comes the pandemic of COVID-19. He had COVID in 2020, around the summer, and I took care of him. He got over it, just like many, he was asymptomatic, and in a few days, he was fine. in December of 2021, we both got COVID. My birthday is Christmas Eve, and we both had Covid this past Christmas. We both had it for well over ten days, I felt better, but Julio was not recovering well. He was extremely ill; I took him to the hospital. I survived, and Julio Cesar Pardo passed away three weeks after he was admitted to the hospital. I lost my love, my passion, my best friend, my confidant, my knight in shining armor. May he forever Rest-In-Peace, the love of my life. How I loved you so. May his memory always be in this book, R.I.P. Julio Cesar Pardo.

The year 2022 was a rough time in my life, as I also lost mother, nine days apart from Julio. She however, lived a long life. Betty Ana Claudio lived to ninety years old, and passed of natural causes. I have for the last eight months, been trying hard and working even harder to get my life back. Honestly, it has been the hardest time in my existence. When I write this book, I'm writing from heart's pain, and life's experience of grief, loss, divorce, past broken relationships, heartache, and much pain. The pages of this book are raw, real, and come from a deep place in my heart called true love. However, I will be writing another book and the full story of Julio's passing of Covid, because we are the survivors of a pandemic, because we are a generation, a people, which are not even spoken about. There is a big difference with a loved one who is ill, or has a disease, but with Covid, you were not allowed to see them or even say your goodbyes. We lost our loved ones unexpectedly, and we could not see them or say our goodbyes, but that's another book.

In essence, I have come, believe it or not, to grow even deeper and stronger than ever before. I had prayed throughout my life, before I met Julio, but once I lost the love of my life, it was then that I really sought and searched for myself. I really sought and did positive affirmations, work on positive living, meditation, and although I did practice it to a normal degree, it now became my survival. I felt lost, abandoned more than ever before, with no one to talk to truly understand me. I got therapy and coaching once a week for months. I said to myself, I need to pray more, meditate more, do more positive affirmations, and do mirror love. I now had to survive for survival to me was not on purpose, to take away my pain. I worked hard, now eight months after the passing of Julio and my mother, now harder than before, as I am grateful to be alive.

I could have died just like Julio, but God, my God, my Universe gave me a second chance to live. I ask myself, "How I was spared? We were together," and I don't have the answers, except to say, "Thank you, God." So, I wrote this book, for my growth, to help others be strong, and become survivors in life, as I am doing it together with you. We must never give up, we must never give in. We must be grateful, thankful, and live each day as if it's our last, and take never take each breath for granted. Be real and raw with yourself, be you, be natural, let your essence shine. Never look at anyone else's achievement with jealousy or envy, but be thankful that they too are given the chance at life. Lastly, exude life each day, for it is as ashes, and let your light so shine, that all will see your light from the rooftops. Stay firm in your convictions, and live your life, be free, be real, be joyous, be courteous, be kinds, be *love*.

I am so thankful to have been given the opportunity and another chance to love and be loved again. Thank you, Julio, for your giving self, your patriotism – it was admirable – your kindness, and that beautiful smile. I pray that from heaven you see and read these words in these pages, which are so full of wisdom and love toward you, my love. Thank you for loving Lola, our dog; she misses you dearly; they know, animals are so smart. My entire family loves and misses you dearly. You put a stamp on all of our hearts. I see your photos and say, "Where did you go?" like you are going to come through the door one day. It is so surreal to me, that to this day, it is only eight months ago, but it feels like you left yesterday. My heart aches, my soul misses you dearly, and I will write these words of love and truth, as you were so deserving of love and admiration. Thank you for making me a better person, a person who learned to love again. You taught me unity, compassion, affection, and to know I always had someone there for me. I still feel your presence at times, and am still working through the pain and loss of you, my love. Until we meet again, I will forever love you, forever and ever into eternity, and into infinity. My Julito, my sweetheart, I love you, more, more, more. God, please take care of my Julito.

MEMORIAM TO COVID-19 FAMILIES

I would like to dedicate these words here and now to the families that lost loved ones to Covid-19. This pandemic came out of nowhere. It hit the world hard and strong. We were left to seclude ourselves, and many human lives were lost. My prayers and condolences go out to each family member, friend, or loved one, that you lost during the pandemic.

I lost my fiancé, Julio Cesar Pardo, R.I.P., to Covid-19. I also lost a few friends and acquaintances. I felt that, on top of all that I lost and gained in life, losing Julito really devastated me. I met Julito at a time in my life when I was finally ready to take a chance at love again. Then, we both got Covid mid-December 2021, right before Christmas. My birthday happens to be Christmas Eve, so for Christmas and my birthday we were both so sick.

I finally noticed that after about two weeks, I began to regain my strength. Julio, on the other hand, did not. He lost all his appetite and seemed very weak. I decided to cook him a nice homemade chicken soup. He sat up and ate it and smiled. He was not talking much. I noticed that day that he had difficulty walking to the bathroom without gasping for air. I suggested let's go to the hospital, he said no, let's call the doctor. So, we made a virtual call to his personal doctor. He immediately said to both of us on the virtual call to immediately take him to the Emergency Room. We went that evening, and the ER was packed with Covid patients, coughing, and very sickly. They finally called him and as soon as they took his vitals, they ran to give him oxygen, it was low. He was admitted that evening. I was told to leave the hospital as it was not safe for me to be there as I could relapse and get Covid again. I cried and left him there with his winter jacket and his cell phone.

I remember driving home. I was lost on the road. I lost my bearing and was driving the opposite way instead of home. I must have passed my exit. I was now on the phone with my sister, and she guided me home. That was the last time I saw Julio conscious. They did all they could for him. I feel the saddest part of a Covid death in a family is that once they went into the hospital, family could not visit. For the first few days, he called me on the phone, and would Facetime me. He was transferred to another hospital that helped Covid patients with an ECMO machine; it's a life and lung support machine. He did not survive the ECMO machine. It was three weeks in the hospital, and he passed away. I'm grateful that his last few hours let me in although he was unconscious in a coma. Some families, they were not allowed in the hospital to say their good-byes. It has been one of the most difficult times of my life. Julio has been gone for eight months. That was such a short time ago.

The way I truly feel is I am still numb; I still cannot believe it. It seems surreal to me that the man that I was going to spend the rest of my life with is not here. I feel for all of those that have lost your loved one to Covid-19. My prayers, love, and condolences to each one of you that has lost a loved one in the pandemic. May you find comfort and peace in your loss.

A LOVE NOTE TO MY READER

Where to go from here? We keep growing, hoping and believing for a better world. We keep striving for a better life. We never, ever give up. My heart and love for you are in these pages, like a love letter to see you grow and change into the flower of beauty you were meant to always be. Always keep in mind to grow in positive aspects. Find ways to feel good about yourself. Remember, you need to come first, in order to be good for anyone else. Never forget to find alone time for self-reflection, prayer, meditation, and those amazing positive affirmations I so much talk about. They have helped me through rough seas. Find the love and freedom with all who you encounter, in all and everything you do. Don't allow the insecurities to seep in, but instead be vigilant, and become secure, as secure as the love that God has for you. Remember, as we discussed, to make sure you surround yourself with positive people, who speak highly of you, and stay clear of those who do not. Live in a positive environment or make changes quickly for the revival of your spirit to come forth.

Just be happy, be vigilant, be aware of your surroundings, that nothing will spoil the fruit of your vine. Find what makes you happy, meditate on that, and most importantly, live in the now, live in the moment. For if you are even believing for some manifestation, some answers to come, don't let the wait get you down. Live life as if you already have the answers, and the manifestations are already on the way. Be joyful, that what you are believing for is already on the way, down the pipe, and no matter what, be grateful for the little things, and even the things you have that you are simply wanting to change. Be thankful for the process. I wrote earlier, as many said, that the blessing is in the journey, not in the destination. It's one of my favorite quotes. I promise this works, and if you allow the pipe of dreams, and of prayers, and the Law of Attraction, positive affirmations, to work, and to become real in your thoughts, they will manifest into reality. They simply must, it is law.

Learn to be still. We run around all the time, we work, we shop for food and things, drive here and there – we need to stop. Stop and allow yourself a breather. How can you analyze anything at all, if you can't even sit still and think? Stay focused, and again I reinforce, stay in the moment, in order to find yourself. We take time to shower and wash up, it's time to wash our mindsets clean, and become whole again. This will give you all the security you need to live a healthy, well-balanced life. We discussed in a previous chapter about forgiving. Forgive – it sets you free. Allow your intuition to rule, don't always go by your heart, your heart can deceive you, like, "Oh, my, how handsome is he?" that's your emotional person speaking. Allow your gut, your intuition to rise up and speak to you. It takes time, to hear your inner-being; you need to learn who your inner-being is, by spending time with her or him, or your Source. How do you hear your intuition, your inner-being? By meditation. Please recall I did speak in detail about this subject. Please refer back when needed. A river of life will flow through your being. Open yourself to new experiences, new avenues of growth.

Keep in mind that life lessons will continue to occur, but with these steps I have laid out, it will become easier to maneuver your experiences in daily living. It is important to enjoy the flow of life, good or bad, in your life experiences. We cannot cave into the winds, storms, and waves of time. Remember they live in the outside of you. That's deep and key to know. This is what is known as living with inner peace and tranquility. All will be alright.

It's time to be brave and put your big girl pants, your heels, and nice jeans, or dress up and be who you have always dreamed to be. Even if others don't understand you, or say she's lost it, good, you have lost it, you lost your past. Amen and hallelujah, it is perfect in your world. Remember, as you meditate, sit there quietly, and let your life flow in your thoughts like a movie – but the difference is, you're the actor. Keep your vitality alive in you, take care of your health and your inner world. Always, abide, abide, abide in your time of meditation. Stop rushing – you can get further on your thoughts, than you can in your car.

LOVE MERCY AND GRACE

Love mercy, grace, and gratitude, and remember to draw from the bank of within. Allow the onion layers to be peeled – it is stinky – but keep going day by day, and night by night, as you continue your journey to greatness. Let freedom reign in your life. I mentioned earlier, let people live and make their own choices, and each of us is responsible for our destinies and consciousness. We are nobody's God, only God is God, and He paid the price for us, and we do not pay a price for anyone else.

I have been recapping in this chapter to solidify the message of the purpose which is my readers' dream come true. We need to have good, keen perception and be persistent in our lives. Take life by the horns. The Bible says be gentle as a dove, but sharp as a lion.

In conclusion, it is going to take a great awakening to

turn your life to the north star, to the true north, facing forward, as the north star faces forward. Take the right road of faith and never stop abiding in your thoughts, prayers, and meditations. When the store clerk calls you and says next, you go, well, it's not just your time, my love, it's your turn, you are next in line for a miracle, and now it is your *turn*, to create a new life for yourself – no more procrastinating and waiting for things to just drop from the sky. It takes work to work on yourself. You got this. Do not leave any stone left unturned, ponder on everything that comes to your mind. It comes to your mind for a reason of healing. Allow the process of thought to play itself out. Be grateful every day for the life that you have, be secure, in your liberty, freedom and power. You hold a power, and that is that no one knows what we are thinking. We hold that power; enjoy that power; I love it. Many times, people think a certain way about us, and they are so wrong, and so off base, I just laugh, because I hold the power behind my head, my brain, my thinking, unless I tell you, you would never know what I am thinking. I just love that gift of internal privacy. Always guard your heart and make an effort to always think highly of yourself. Remember, I mentioned that if a bad thought comes, throw it out, right in the garbage. Don't give those thoughts a second longer in your thinking, and that my friends, is another power you have, the power to change your minds, at the drop of a hat. I love that so much, because I'm free and I will decide my destiny. We don't have to be egotistical about it, but use that change your mind tool, if you need to, and please be free, do not feel guilty, and that is the power of freedom at work.

My vision for you, my readers, is to be whole, happy, free, and blessed. I have given steps and keys and benefits here. Stay in the winner's circle and be grateful and thankful daily. All the gifts of life are yours for the taking.

Some may have difficulty and say, "That's for someone else." No, it's for everyone, and if you don't believe it, you will not grow and achieve your destiny. Change your mind-set, which is easy to do – just do it – and watch what happens. What you believe, speak, and think will be your ability in which changes will occur and you will then grow into your destiny. It's called God, the Universe, your higher power, your inner-self – and it is the wonderful and incredible Law of Attraction. It's real, and it's yours for the asking. Be happy, be free, be you. Only believe, and you will see the glory of God.

"Therefore if the son make you free, you shall be free indeed."

— JOHN 8:34, NKJV

IN A DISTANCE

Poem in Memory and Dedication to Julio Cesar Pardo, R.I.P.

In a distance,
I see you, like a ray of sunshine,
Gleaming through the trees
Your love surrounds me,
A light, like a beam
Tears streaming down my face,
I thank God for the love you gave,
And when I see you again,
I know it would have been, only by his grace
Days go by,
I know you're well,
Oh, what stories would you tell
For me, I would tell of our love,
I'd give people hope,
And say, it's not the end of the rope.

— MYRNA IVETTE CLAUDIO

ACKNOWLEDGMENTS

I would love to thank my God, my Source, my Universe, and my guide, and for helping me co-create this book. I thank You forever for Your love, strength, and courage that You so bountifully give me daily. I so appreciate the journey and experience I am on, and for guiding me to find my full potential. I will be sure to always give You all the praise, honor, and glory due to Your name, and to lift Your name before all creation. I love You; I praise You, and I thank You!

I bountifully give thanks to Dr. Angela Lauria, founder and CEO. Your entire team are rock stars at the Author Incubator. Thanks to Paul Brycock, Madeline Kosten, Karmi Koen, Lisa Steele, Danielle Felton, Jennifer Stimson, the entire team, for their amazing work, effort, and support, and you all do it with incredible wisdom and superb knowledge. Thank you for your excellent accountability, and tough love to help me write and finish this book.

Thank you, Angela, for being that angel that came into my life for the specific purpose of birthing my book into the world. I am forever grateful. Your program and coaching are unique like none other. Your intelligence just beams like a light in a dark world, you made my dreams come true. You taught me so much through your weekly calls, videos, and the amazing love and support you gave me and all the authors past.

Thank you to the Editor-In-Chief, Madeline Kosten, who was with me from the beginning and always helped me with any questions I had. Your kindness and support are impeccable. I will always be grateful to you for your guidance throughout this entire process. You are truly one sweet and special woman. You truly are one of a kind. I will forever be grateful to you.

A special thank you to my Managing Editor, Cory Hott, for making my book journey amazing and for being such a positive human being. You beam like a ray of light, full of glory, and joy, and your light always shone, throughout the entire process. You were a dream to work with, and I learned so much with your guidance and intellect about creating a better book. I appreciate the patience and encouragement you constantly gave to me throughout the process. Thank you, Cory, for not just being an incredible, intelligent, brilliant editor, but for helping me every step of the way, from day one of the edits, to the finish, and the publishing of the book. I am so thankful, grateful, and happy you got me to the finish line. Bravo, and thank you!

A special thanks to my photographers for the photos in this book, Attreo Santayana, and RP, from LinkedInHead shots.com, for your beautiful work, expertise, quality of not just time spent, but of your work. This really made the difference in my personal life. You are amazing! Thank you both at LinkedInHeadshotsNYC.com.

A special thanks to my personal Modeling Photographer, Attreo Santayana, from MAGS Studios, for all the wonderful photos, your patience, great photoshoot, and I am certainly looking forward to more amazing photo shoots. A special thanks, my friend! facebook.com/attreophotography.

Angel Luis Claudio, and Betty Ana Claudio, my mom and dad, I know you are going to receive these words in Heaven above. I see a lot of both of you whenever I look in the mirror, and that makes me so proud to be called your daughter. I hope you can look down and are proud of me, as I have written the pages of this book for the people who have endured broken hearts. I pray the angels carry this acknowledgment love letter right into both your hands. Thank you for the love and example you showed me as my parents. May the love you shared on earth continue in Heaven. Papi, as you always said to all of us, I love you more, more, more, so now, I say it back to both of you. I love you, Mami and Papi, more, more, more! Papi as you always called me, Minufin, and I will have that in my heart forever, and Mami, thank you for being the strong and courageous woman that you were. You taught me to be strong and to never give up. I love you both forever and into eternity more, more, more!

Julio Cesar Pardo, my forever love, I ask the angels again, to carry these words as a love letter to you in Heaven. You, my fiancé on earth, are now in Heaven. I want to thank you for bringing a bright light and love into my life. I enjoyed every single moment we were together. I will never, ever forget your charismatic wit, your laughter, and your incredible intelligence. You remembered dates, birthdays, anniversaries, even dates that most would not even remember. I truly thank God for the time we shared together. I told you, Julito, I would write a book, and you encouraged me, and believed in me. Well, here it is, my love! Please read it from Heaven and blow me a kiss down to earth, so I know you did. I will forever love you until eternity and into infinity. Your Reina, Nenita, I always love you, and I promise, we will forever dance again, when we meet again at Heaven's gates. I will forever love you, more, more, more!

My sons, Ronnie, Leo, and Michael Sean, thank you so very much for being the lights in my life. I am so extremely proud of you – you are all such hard working, loving, and kindhearted sons, husbands, and fathers. Mama is so immensely proud of the three of you. A mother's desire is always to see their children happy, healthy, and living successful lives. Well, you have superseded that, and I know you are always achieving to be better. Life is not easy, but you all roll with the punches, and that is growth right there. Continue to grow, stay aligned, stay positive, meditate, pray, stay alert, enlightened, learning, seeking knowledge, working hard, being faithful, loving, and staying as the impressive men that you have become. Never change, only get better! Ronnie, Leo, and Michael Sean, you are my life, you are my world, never forget that I live for you, and Mama is so very blessed and proud of all of you. I love you more, more, more. Forever and ever, your Mama, more, more, more, than you will ever know!

Jamie, Melissa, and Lauren, my three beautiful daughters-in-laws, I want to thank you first for loving my sons, the way that you do and for taking care of them and yourselves, and the children, and for making my sons so happy and secure. I know they adore each one of you. Jamie, you are so meticulously loving, it is admirable. You amaze me with your beauty and strength. I am so enormously proud of you and blessed to have you as my daughter. Thank you for being you! Thank you for loving my son, Ronnie, and the children, Austin Luis, and Brooklyn Angelina. You are an incredible nurturing mother. I have never seen Ronnie as happy as he is with you. I am intently aware that you lost both your parents recently, and I want you to know I promised them both, before they passed away, that I would take care of you. I am so blessed to have you in our family. You are so beautiful. I want you to know I love you very much, deeply, and will do my best to do so. I promise I will always love you as my own. Thank you again for loving my son and family the way you do. Thank you again Jamie, I love you so, your Mama, more, more, more than you will ever know!

In loving memory to Jaime's, my daughter-in-law's,

parents, Allan and Bobby Borack. We love and miss you so very much. This has not been easy for my daughter-in-law Jamie, losing her parents, but I promise you, I will forever make sure that you know how much I love you! Allan was a wonderful man, great husband, and father. Bobby was spunky and never took her NCIS hat off. She loved her TV show. They would be so proud of you, Jamie and Ronnie, and the beautiful parents you have become to Austin Luis and Brooklyn Angelina. They are watching and pouring love on you Jamie and Ronnie, Austin, and Brooklyn, from heaven above!

Melissa, thank you for loving my son Leo the way that you do. Also, thank you so very much for being the person that you are, and I know why my son fell in love with you the minute he met you. Even before he met you, he loved you. I have never seen Leo as happy as he is with you. You are an amazing, caring, loving, nurturing woman, a true and amazing family girl, and an amazing businessperson. I am so immensely proud to call you my daughter, and I am so lucky and blessed you are in our family. I know how much you love to travel, how much you love the Caribbean and the beach – you and me, we both have that in common. I know you will make an amazing mother one day. You are so intelligent, witty, and beautiful. I love you, and I thank you again, for loving my son the way that you do. I promise you I will always love you as my own. Thank you again, Melissa, I love you so, Mama, more, more, more than you will ever know!

Lauren, thank you for loving my son Michael Sean the way that you do. I admire the way you love motherhood, and how wonderful you are as a mother to your precious daughter, Antonia Marie. You truly are an amazing woman; you're beautiful, and so incredibly nurturing. Thank you for loving your stepson, Adrian Jiovanni, AJ, the way you do. You have such a lovely family. You are a beautiful teacher, mother, wife, and I am so proud to call you my daughter. I have never seen Michael Sean so happy as he is with you. I am so blessed that you and Antonia came into our lives and are now a part of our family, and I promise you I will always love you as my own. Thank you again, Lauren, I love you so, Mama, more, more, more than you will ever know!

I want to give a special thank you to Melissa's mom and dad, Mike, and Louise, for being such dedicated and wonderful parents to Melissa and her brother and sisters. Especially for raising such a beautiful family. Your daughter is classy, intelligent, and a brilliant young woman, who married my son Leo, also known as Sergeant Leonard Stephen Anthony, US Marine Corps.

I want to give a special thank you to Lauren's mom and dad, Andy, and Margarita for being such dedicated and wonderful parents to Lauren and her sister. Especially for raising such a beautiful family. Your daughter is classy, intelligent, and a brilliant young woman, who will marry my son Michael Sean.

Isabella Marie, my first granddaughter, it was such a delight taking care of you as you grew up as a little girl, and now you have grown to be such a beautiful young woman. I am so genuinely proud of the person you have grown to be. Since the day you were born, you brought a special light into my life: that light is you. You are beautiful, my gorgeous granddaughter. I love you so, so very much! Thank you for your loving support. You are so beautiful, sweet spirited, intelligent, and talented. I am amazed at the creative juices that flow through you, and the artist you have become. I am always in awe of your artwork. You have become an entrepreneur, and an amazing businessperson. Sweetheart, the world is your oyster, so and take charge of your life, more blessings are on the horizon for you, they are there for the picking. Always stay alert, away from the negative, stay positive, and be happy! Thank you again for being you, and know I love you more, more, more than you will ever know!

Adrian Jiovanni, AJ, my first grandson, thank you for your kind heart. I am so glad when we spoke about my book, you said, as I was driving you home one night, from a family get together, you were interested and asked questions, like what it was about, and that made me so happy, that you were interested in what Grandma was doing. Thank you for your love and support. I am so glad you love school, and you enjoy playing your video games, and going outside to the park and hanging out with your friends. It makes me so happy and your dad, and family, to see that you love your family and friends. I know you cannot wait for your dad and Lauren's wedding. I am so extremely proud of you, and the young man you have become. You light up our world! It thrills me to know that when you get older, you still want to be an architect. Your dad, Michael, said, you have been saying that since you were three years old. I am so happy you are into school and are getting good grades. Your entire family is enormously proud of you. Thank you for everything, for who you are. Stay true to yourself, stay away from negativity, always be positive, always be alert, and continue this amazing path you are on. The world is your oyster, my grandson! Never forget like Grandma Betty used to always tell you, and me too, that I love you more, more, more than you will ever know!

Antonia Marie, thank you so very much for always being the light in the room. You are a diamond, shining brightly every day. Since I met you, you shone and lit up the room. Your essence and beauty are amazing. You are incredibly smart, and I am so immensely proud of you. You are such a beautiful and intelligent young girl. We are all so proud of you. Mom mentioned how she and all of us are all always so fascinated by how talented you are with your sketching, drawing, coloring, paint, and imagination. Your creativity, empathy, heart, smarts, style, and smile brighten every day. I always look forward to our family times together. I am immensely proud to call you my granddaughter. I love you more, more, more than you will ever know!

Austin Luis, my sweet and adorable grand baby boy. I love it when you shout out da da da, like you are singing it to the world. I love it when your head turns sideways so I can tickle you under your neck and stomach. You are your mom and dad's treasure. You go in circles in the living room and kitchen, and around again, and you light up the room, my beautiful grandson! At nineteen months, you are not walking but running. I was there with you at your first Yankee game; what a thrill we all had, partaking in that event. You are so precious, and Nina loves you, more, more, more than you will ever know!

Brooklyn Angelina, my new baby granddaughter, I wanted to write something special about you. You are a very blessed little angel, and little mermaid. You have a beautiful family, Daddy Ronnie, and mama Jaime, who adore you so very, very much. You have a brother Austin Luis, who will love and protect you all the days of your life. You are our little mermaid. Your dad has worked endless hours to get your beautiful mermaid room ready; it is beautiful, with a chandelier, stars on the curtains, and purple accented walls. As I write this, you are only a week old today. We love you more, more, more than you will ever know!

Madeleine and Tony, I want to thank you for your love and support, especially throughout the loss of Julito, your brother-in-law, this year. I will always appreciate you both, thank you! It was a very trying time losing Mom and Julio nine days apart from each other. It was not easy going through that time of grief and suffering. Thank you to your family for the part they shared in making his Memorial Service memorable. I am forever grateful. Thank you, again, Madeleine, for all you personally did on behalf of our mother, Betty Ana Claudio, may she rest in peace. R.I.P. I want to acknowledge especially the fact that you were there with me hours before Julio's passing and I could not ever do that alone. We were all in pins and needles. I will forever be grateful that you were with me. Again, thank you genuinely so much. Your strength amid all the pain was incredible. I love you more, more, more!

Elizabeth and David, thank you for the love and strength you showed me at the passing of your brother-in-law to be Julito. Elizabeth thank you also for being there for me throughout this journey this past year, you have been an anchor of love. I will never forget that you flew from Phoenix, Arizona to be with us here for his funeral services. Thank you, Elizabeth, for sharing your beautiful song, The Prayer, just impeccable and you so sang it so lovely. Thank you, David, my wonderful brother-in-law, for the friendship you shared with Julio, and for doing his eulogy. It was so very personal and so very touching, we cried with you. Elizabeth, thank you for being a case study, as you shared your personal experience and growth, in this book, in Chapter 9. Your words will help a sea of people around the globe that are hurting from broken relationships. The mission of this book is to bring light to those who suffer from brokenness. Losing Mom, as well, was not easy, but your incredible courage and strength, you got from her, was endearing. You carry her light, wherever you go, so thank you, I love you more, more, more!

To my Nancy, my forever bestie cousin, you are my life-line on this earth. My bestest cousin, my confidant, my prayer partner, and we are prayer warriors! Without you, I would have no one to bounce things off with. When you are happy, I am happy. You have been a treasure to me since you began to crawl. I made sure I took you out of the playpen to play with me. I was close to ten years old, and you were just starting to walk. I got in so much trouble, and as soon as the grownups walked away, I would do it again, I would take you out of the playpen. I did not care, we had fun playing together. Thank you for being there hours prior to Julio's passing, and when he passed, we went back to see him one last time to say our goodbyes. Thank you, Nancy, for being with me throughout the entire process, and even in the writing of this book, as I have bounced ideas back and forth, you have encouraged me tremendously. My Nancy, my love, my bestest cousin, I adore you! You are simply gorgeousness! I am so proud of the woman and mother that you are, I know it has not been easy for you as well, as you recently lost your mama, my Aunt Doris, mi Titi Doris, remember, I am always here for you! Thank you for all the time of sharing, caring, and praying! Thank you! I love you more, more, more!

To my entire family – in Puerto Rico, and throughout the states, and around the world – I love you dearly. From aunts, uncles, cousins, second cousins, nieces, nephews, my madrina, Myrna, on both sides of the family. My words could never express my love and gratitude for you. I could never in words express the love I have for you. Just because we are separated by miles, remember that distance could never keep you far from my thoughts, and my heart. There is not one day that I do not think of you and pray for you. I love you all dearly, mi bella familia, los adoro con todo mi Corazón!

I want to give a special thanks to my friends from work. Christina, Janet, Ana, Jeffrey, Samantha, and Kevin, thank you for always being there for me. You are what I call true and beautiful friends. Your support and friendship mean the world to me. I am so happy you are in my life. Thank you also to my co-workers Ginny, Cielo, Jordan, Teisha, and Julissa for being so supportive when my fiancé, Julio Cesar Pardo, R.I.P., passed away this year, 2022. Your support and care meant everything to me. Thank you and I appreciate and love you all!

This woman is beautiful inside and out, my Ceyla. I love you to pieces. Thank you for always being there for me and helping me, especially with the help you gave me in the care of my mother, Betty Ana Claudio, when she was living with me and my family in Long Island, NY. You are always there for me, whenever I need you the most! I will never forget that. You are one of a kind! Ceyla, you are the most giving and loving person I have ever known. I love you and Felipe, and Felipe, I am so sorry you lost your dad to Covid, and Ceyla, sorry for the recent loss of your mother also. I dearly love you. Thank you always, y los adoro con todo mi corazon!

Thank you to my little social butterfly, Charmaine. Thank you for always being there for me. You are my Jamaican sister, we share the same age, and we both lost our mates to Covid-19. You have been a blessing in my life, and always make me laugh so hard. I am sorry for your husband Leslie's loss to Covid and know that I will always be there for you. Thank you for being there for me.

Thank you to my cruising friends, Cliff and Violetta. What fun times we had! I will never forget you and the wonderful Caribbean cruise we had. We are forever friends, and I look forward to our next ocean adventure in the high seas! Love you dearly!

Thank you to my amazing and beautiful friend Celine. Thank you for always reaching out to me; even when I was gone for years, you found me. You are a gem and will forever be my best friend. Best friends for life! I love you, blessings to you and Mike forever!

Thank you to the Pardo family in Colombia, Julio's

R.I.P., family in his native country. Julietica, thank you for your love and support, for always reaching out to me. I love our communication! I know how close you and your brother were. Thank you, Julietica, for being there for me like a real sister. My sincere thank you to Fernando, Dario, and Ivan, for coming to New York, and being with me at your brother and uncle's passing. Fernandito, what you did for your brother, Julio, and for me was out of pure love! Fernandito, I will always love you dearly! Your presence and all your help, especially with the storage unit, and cleaning out his things from the room, I could never have done this without you. I will never forget you and all you did, and I thank you! I will forever be grateful for your love and support in such a tough time. Thank you to the rest of the Pardo siblings, nieces, nephews, cousins, and the entire Pardo family. I will forever pray I can still be a part of your amazing family. The sadness we have all experienced from this tragedy has brought us closer, and it has not been easy, but we keep on moving forward, that is what Julio would want for all of us. Thank you all outside of the family for being there for me in such a tough time. It was only ten months ago, and it is still so fresh. May God continue to heal us all. Thank you familia Pardo, los adoro con todo mi corazon!

Thank you, Elizabeth, Lina, Lucille, Margaret, and Celine, for your input in this book, which made this book even more special. The stories that you shared about your personal lives, although not easy, what you went through, will forever help others heal and come to their full blessed potential. I know God will use your words for the benefit of healing the readers that have endured suffering, loneliness, verbal or physical abuse, hurt, rejection, loss of self-worth, identity crisis, insecurities, abandonment, and pain, around the world. Broken lives will be mended because of your contribution to this project, this book, *Life After Him.*

ABOUT THE AUTHOR

Myrna Ivette Claudio is a certified life coach, SAG-AFTRA actress, model, Latin dancer, gospel singer, ordained Evangelist, Revivalist, and the founder of a Bible Teaching Ministry, where for years she produced a local, Long Island, New York, Christian Television Production, and did extensive Christian Counseling for more than twenty-five years.

She has a heart to help people feel better about themselves, and a desire to help them build stronger mindsets. She is most known for her passion and love of life, God, family, and humanity. She shares an ardent desire to bring out the best in people, and to see them reach their full potential. She wants nothing more than to see them come from brokenness to wholeness. She is devoted to empowering growth of emotional, spiritual wellbeing, and stability. She is determined to share her life's experiences with as many people as possible.

When Myrna Ivette is not writing, she likes to read, dance Latin salsa and merengue, take walks on the beach, and dine out. She loves to travel, loves cooking, wine tastings, taking road trips, going to Yankee games, football, and loves the Knicks, writing poetry, listening to positive videos, blogging, taking selfies, and enjoys going to see a good Broadway show. In her daily routine, she does meditation, prayer, positive affirmations, journaling, and exercising.

Her secret passion is spending time with her children and grandchildren. She is the mother of three grown sons, Ronnie, Leo, and Michael Sean, all with beautiful wives and children. She is the daughter of Angel Luis and Betty Ana Claudio, who are now looking down from heaven. She is one of three girls, the middle one, they call her, and loves her two sisters Madeleine and Elizabeth, and the entire family dearly. She is a native of the Island of Enchantment, Puerto Rico, with Indigenous background, and descendance from Spain, Portuguese, Israel, and France. Myrna Ivette is a snowbird and resides in both Long Island, New York, and Miami Beach, Florida.

Website: www.myrnaivetteclaudio.com

Email: authorinfo@myrnaivetteclaudio.com

Facebook: https://www.facebook.com/Myrna-IvetteClaudio

Instagram: @myrnaivette1224

ABOUT DIFFERENCE PRESS

Difference Press is the publishing arm of The Author Incubator, an Inc. 500 award-winning company that helps business owners and executives grow their brand, establish thought leadership, and get customers, clients, and highly-paid speaking opportunities, through writing and publishing books.

While traditional publishers require that you already have a large following to guarantee they make money from sales to your existing list, our approach is focused on using a book to grow your following – even if you currently don't have a following. This is why we charge an up-front fee but never take a percentage of revenue you earn from your book.

☞ MORE THAN A COACH. MORE THAN A PUBLISHER. ✍

We work intimately and personally with each of our authors to develop a revenue-generating strategy for the book. By using a Lean Startup style methodology, we guarantee the book's success before we even start writing. We provide all the technical support authors need with editing, design, marketing, and publishing, the emotional support you would get from a book coach to help you manage anxiety and time constraints, and we serve as a strategic thought partner engineering the book for success.

The Author Incubator has helped almost 2,000 entrepreneurs write, publish, and promote their non-fiction books. Our authors have used their books to gain international media exposure, build a brand and marketing following, get lucrative speaking engagements, raise awareness of their product or service, and attract clients and customers.

☞ ARE YOU READY TO WRITE A BOOK? ✍

As a client, we will work with you to make sure your book gets done right and that it gets done quickly. The Author Incubator provides one-stop for strategic book consultation, author coaching to manage writer's block and anxiety, full-service professional editing, design, and self-publishing services, and book marketing and launch campaigns. We sell this as one package so our clients are not slowed down with contradictory advice. We have a 99 percent success rate with nearly all of our clients completing their books, publishing them, and reaching bestseller status upon launch.

☞ APPLY NOW AND BE OUR NEXT SUCCESS STORY ✍

To find out if there is a significant ROI for you to write a book, get on our calendar by completing an application at www.TheAuthorIncubator.com/apply.

OTHER BOOKS BY DIFFERENCE PRESS

Profitable Salon Owner: Rise Above the Chaos In Your Business and Reignite Your Passion and Profits by Jason Everett

Leadership Recreated: A Woman's Guide to Surviving and Thriving in Patriarchal Academia by Kem Gambrell, Ph.D.

Happy Gay Christian Hereafter: 8 Steps to Reconcile Your Identity to Family and Faith or Leave without Regret by Carter Neill Holmes

Talk More, Fight Less: Rebuilding, Renewing, and Restoring Communication in Your Relationship by Dr. Sandra W. Ingram

Starting and Serving: Your Personal Guide to Launching a Successful, New Career as a Nonprofit Leader by R. Romona Jackson, Esq.

The Photographer's Path: Do What You Love, Tell Client's Stories through Images, and Have the Business of Your Dreams by Maya Manseau

Marathon in the Fog: Supporting a Parent with Dementia in Life and Death by Jennifer Olden, LMFT

THANK YOU

Thanks for taking the time to read my book, *Life after Him*. I pray it has been an encouragement to you. My desire in these pages is to bring out the best in you, as a new day, and a new awakening arises. My heart's desire is for you to reach your full destiny and potential. Here in these pages, are my love letter to you, as I poured out my heart and soul. As a personal gift to you, I have created a companion video for you to watch, that goes along with this book. Visit my website below anytime to watch the companion video. If you would like to contact me, you can do so by shooting me an email. Once again, I sincerely thank you! Be free, be happy, be you, stay positive, and be blessed.

— Myrna Ivette Claudio

Website: www.myrnaivetteclaudio.com

Email: authorinfo@myrnaivetteclaudio.com